THE
HISTORICAL JESUS
IN THE
GOSPEL OF ST JOHN

W9-ADD-608

ABOUT THE BOOK

The problem raised by the discrepancy between the synoptic gospels' treatment of Jesus and that of the fourth gospel has bewildered readers of the New Testament from the Patristic era to the present. The Gospel of St John is a distinctive interpretation of the words and deeds of Jesus written from a highly personal point of view. The precise determination of the nature of that point of view and of its historical character is a matter of hermeneutics; and it is the signal achievement of Franz Mussner in explaining that nature to have drawn upon the insights of Heidegger in an analysis of such Johannine terms as "to see", "to hear", "to testify", and "to remember". The author concludes that St John's historical perspective is that of a believing witness who in remembrance *sees* his subject in such a way that the hidden mystery of Jesus of Nazareth becomes visible and expressible for the Church in the kerygma.

QUAESTIONES DISPUTATAE

FRANZ MUSSNER

THE
HISTORICAL JESUS
IN THE
GOSPEL OF ST JOHN

"Finally John, recognizing that the 'bodily facts'
had been treated in the (synoptic) gospels, . . .
inspired by the Spirit, wrote a 'spiritual' gospel."
Clement of Alexandria according to Eusebius,
Ecclesiastical History, VI, 14, 7.

HERDER FREIBURG

PALM PUBLISHERS
MONTREAL

226.506
Mott

Original edition :
" Die Johanneische Sehweise und die Frage nach dem historischen Jesus ",
Herder, Freiburg, 1965. Translated by W. J. O'HARA.

Nihil Obstat: Lionel Swain, S.T.L., L.S.S.

Censor deputatus

Imprimatur: ✠Patritius Casey, Vic. Gen.

Westmonasterii, die 22ª Septembris 1966

The Nihil Obstat and Imprimatur are a declaration that a book or pamphlet is considered to be free from doctrinal or moral error. It is not implied that those who have granted the Nihil Obstat and Imprimatur agree with the contents, opinions or statements expressed.

First published in West Germany © 1967, Herder KG

Printed in the Republic of Ireland by Cahill & Co., Ltd.
PALM PUBLISHERS, 1949—55th Ave., Dorval, Montreal.

CONTENTS

CONTENTS

I

THE PROBLEM

The Johannine Christ speaks differently from the Christ of the synoptics; he speaks John's language. That is an indubitable fact which can be verified by anyone in a position to consult a Greek concordance. The Paraclete sayings alone would serve as conclusive proof.[1] This fact raises even more acutely, and in a form peculiar to the Gospel according to John, the question, widely discussed at the present time, of the "historical" Jesus. To what extent is the Johannine Christ "identical" with the historical Jesus of Nazareth? Should the *Vita Jesu* which the fourth evangelist presents not rather be termed (even if in an elevated sense) a novel about Jesus? A host of other questions are likewise involved, including that of the nature of inspiration. As the discussion about the Jesus of history shows, questions of that kind arise even in regard to the synoptic tradition concerning Jesus,[2] but they become perceptibly more acute in regard to the fourth gospel, especially in view of the discourses of Christ, which are typically "Johannine" in language, style and themes. Who is really speaking there?

These questions set the exegete special problems which are not easily solved, yet urgently call for solution. Experience shows that a satisfactory solution to the whole set of questions cannot be found as long as detailed problems alone are envisaged, such as, for example, the question of the origin of the Johannine tradition. A more radical approach must be made to the problem. Possible access to a solution seems to present itself if the Johannine "mode of vision" or "perspective" is more closely examined. How does the fourth evangelist actually "see" his subject Jesus Christ? Since he uses a particular gnoseological terminology in his gospel and precisely in regard to his historical subject, we are in a position to form some conception of the way he sees things, his mode of vision. If this is taken in conjunction with the position of the fourth gospel in the development of theology, it is possible to determine the hermeneutical situation in which its author was placed. It becomes apparent that the Johannine mode of vision implies a certain interpretative understanding, so that the question: How does John see his subject? is at the same time the question: How does John interpret and understand his subject, Jesus Christ? And only when these questions are answered is it possible to answer correctly the question: Which Christ is it who is standing before us here and speaking?

Understood in this way the "Johannine problem" is chiefly a hermeneutical one. Considerable light and help can be had from the discussions and results of modern hermeneutics, as these have been pursued and achieved in particular by Martin Heidegger (*Sein und Zeit*) in the footsteps of W. Dilthey and, in succession to both, by Hans-Georg Gadamer in his important work *Wahrheit und Methode*.[3] The author of the present essay must confess that it was only his acquaintance with Gadamer's work that gave him courage to examine more closely the Johannine mode of vision and to put forward the results of his work as a *quaestio disputata*. It need hardly be said that a *quaestio disputata* of this kind can only be an attempt to make some headway with a difficult problem. If any success has been achieved, this could form the basis of further research.

II

THE HERMENEUTICAL SITUATION OF THE
FOURTH EVANGELIST

*1. The place of the Gospel according to John in theological
development*

In the general introductions to New Testament studies, the
Gospel according to John is considered the latest of the New
Testament writings, and is assigned to a date between A.D. 90
and 100.[1] It is the fourth Life of Jesus Christ of the canonical
gospels. The synoptic gospels had already been in existence
for 20 to 30 years when John wrote his gospel. The question
arises, as I have already indicated in another connection,[2]
why John wrote a fourth life of Christ at all at the end of
the century, at a time when the writing of gospels in the
Church seemed to be long since at an end. What prompted
him to do so? It is still possible to some extent to give an
answer, if the character of the fourth gospel is examined. It
shows itself to be largely a polemical work. John is evidently
dealing with various opponents and opinions, such as followers
of the Baptist,[3] the Jews (perhaps also heretical Jewish
Christians) and especially Gnostic-Docetist circles. As can also
be seen from the First Letter of John, the controversies with
the latter chiefly concerned Christology, and in particular the

question which has once again become topical today: Are (the crucified) Jesus and the heavenly Christ (the redeemer) identical? The heretics seem to have asserted that Jesus Christ did not really "appear in the flesh" as was taught "from the beginning" in the Church (cf. especially 1 Jn 2:22–24; 4:2 f.); he did not reveal himself in water and blood (cf. 5:6).[4] Consequently they were undermining the Church's Christology which rested on apostolic tradition. Now John not only gave expression to his aims in the form of letters, but also expounded them positively for the Church in the shape of a new *Vita Jesu* as we have it in the fourth gospel. For this gospel is of course quite clearly a new sketch of the life of Jesus, almost completely independent of the synoptics on the literary plane, but quite definitely a new outline prompted by the historical state of theology in the Church at the end of the century. The attack on the apostolic Christology called for a new legitimate and orthodox exposition of the history of Jesus, the programme of which was formulated in Jn 1:14: "And the *Logos* was made flesh"—clearly a polemical statement—"and pitched his tent among us, and we have seen his glory". The programme carried out in the gospel is to testify that Jesus Christ is the incarnate Logos, both Logos and incarnate, in one; and at the same time that his *doxa* became visible in Jesus Christ for the apostolic eye-witnesses among whom the author includes himself.[5]

Whatever may be said of the purpose of the fourth gospel, its author at all events was placed with his Life of Christ in a special hermeneutical situation. He had to concern himself with a figure whose death had occurred more than 60 years before. Moreover, he had to present that figure and his work in such a way that this exposition provided an answer to the Christological questions which had arisen in the Church in the author's time. To put it briefly, he had to answer for the Church the question: Who was Jesus Christ "in actual fact"? Even if in order to answer this question he could refer back to the previous tradition of the Church's belief and its tradition concerning Jesus (see Section VI on this), he nevertheless found himself in a position which, as compared with that of the synoptics, had become more acute, for he was in the position of the historian who is already at least 60 years distant from his "hero". In that way a special problem of hermeneutics arises for the fourth gospel, namely: What part is played in historical interpretative understanding by lapse of time? No doubt this problem already exists in connection with the synoptic historiography but it becomes more acute with John because the time interval was much greater and especially because John was not a compiler (redactor) of the previous tradition of the Church concerning Jesus in the same way as the synoptics were, as form-history has shown; his Life of Jesus is his own project to quite a different extent. In that way the historical perspective in which John wrote his work was also different. What consequences result from this for his hermeneutical situation?

2. Hermeneutical significance of lapse of time and perspective

Lapse of time has hermeneutical significance.[6] That is true not only of later understanding of historical texts, of our understanding of John's gospel, for example, but it is also and particularly true *mutatis mutandis* of someone who is describing an historical figure, as John was with Jesus Christ. The time interval for John was of a special kind. He had not of course a detached, distant relation to his subject but stood in the living tradition of the Church's faith. His position in the development of theology did not indeed require him to dissociate himself from his subject, but it did require detachment in the form of theological reflection on Jesus Christ. At the same time this distance was provided by the great interval of time which separated him from the historical Jesus. Gadamer speaks of "an intermediate position between detached objectivity intended as that of historical inquiry and connection with a tradition. This intermediate position is the truly hermeneutical one".[7] Such an intermediate position provided some of the essential conditions of John's mode of vision, which of course at the same time was an interpretative understanding. Understanding, however, is more than the reproduction of past events. Since John endeavoured with the help of the inspiration of the Spirit of God to penetrate more deeply into the mystery of Jesus and previous tradition concerning him, his understanding of Jesus's person and work and of the tradition concerning them became a productive process. In this way the lapse of time became a positive and creative possibility of understanding.[8] John was not faced with the task of overcoming the interval of time and as it were of jumping back to the historical Jesus; the time interval was no "yawning abyss but was filled by that continuity of origin and tradition, in the light of which all that is handed down exhibits itself to us" (Gadamer). The time interval also existed, of course, for the heretics whom John was opposing. But in contrast to the

13

apostle and evangelist, the heretic, according to 2 John 9 is a
προάγων, a "progressive", who is not concerned about tradition or, as John says in the same passage, does not "abide" in
the (apostolic) διδαχὴ τοῦ Χριστοῦ. As a result the heretic's
hermeneutical undertaking is merely arbitrary: he interprets
Jesus Christ to suit his private gnosis. As modern hermeneutics
recognizes, understanding depends on prior judgments,
presuppositions; that holds good in the present case both of
John and of his Christological opponents. The true and correct
presuppositions are furnished for John both by his own status
as eye-witness and hearer (cf. Jn 1:14; 19:35; 1 Jn 1:1, 3)
and by the previous tradition of the Church's faith. Since the
heretic is no eye-witness and expressly rejects tradition, the
time interval leads in his case to a false conception of the figure
and work of Jesus. In other words, tradition creates for
interpretative understanding a horizon which is an essential
constituent of the concept of an hermeneutical situation.[9]
"The horizon is the range of vision which comprises and
includes all that is visible from a point" (Gadamer). An
historical horizon is not obtained by "putting oneself back"
into an historical situation. The temptation arises, of course,
of explaining the hermeneutical situation of the fourth
evangelist by saying that he put himself into Jesus's position
and even into his "soul", perhaps with the help of an "act of
divination" (of the kind Schleiermacher assumed as a postu-
late in his hermeneutics). Modern hermeneutics has recognized
that one must already have an horizon oneself in order to put
oneself into a situation in that way. Gadamer says: "Such
self-transference is neither one individuality's feeling its way
into another nor a subjecting of the other to one's own

standards, but always signifies a rising to a higher level of generality . . ." [10] A genuinely historical awareness cannot leave out of account its own present. John looks back into the past of the historical Jesus from his own present, that is to say, from the situation in theological development of the time at which he is writing. Its problems are mirrored in the way in which he envisages his historical subject. The encounter with the past and with tradition is prompted by the questions of the present. And so his hermeneutical situation is characterized by a peculiar merging of the two horizons of present and past. "Understanding", says Gadamer, "is always a process of merging two such supposedly independent horizons." [11] The hermeneutical task consists then not of "covering up by naïve assimilation, but of consciously unfolding" the tension that prevails between the different horizons, that is to say, placing the past, which means in the case of the fourth evangelist the historical figure of Jesus of Nazareth, in the correct light on the basis of the questions of the present. The historical horizon is not thereby pushed away into unreality, but only then fully appears and finds expression. The manifold dimensions of the figure of Jesus stand out and its essence persists into the present. [12] Gadamer concludes, "The projection of the historical horizon is therefore only one phase and factor in the accomplishment of understanding and does not harden into alienation from self into a past consciousness, but is attained from one's own horizon of understanding in the present. In the accomplishment of understanding a real merging of horizons takes place."

Now we are in the fortunate position of being able to some degree to analyse the Johannine process of merging of perspectives in this way. John uses a special gnoseological terminology which makes possible an analysis of his "historical reason" and gives us a glimpse into the mode of his understanding of Jesus, so that the mystery of Jesus can disclose itself through the evangelist for his readers too.

III

ANALYSIS OF THE "HISTORICAL REASON" OF THE FOURTH EVANGELIST BY MEANS OF HIS GNOSEOLOGICAL TERMINOLOGY

By his situation in the development of theology, John faced the hermeneutical task of "understanding" Jesus. He aimed at presenting that understanding to the Church of his time in the form of a gospel life of Jesus Christ. But Jesus was separated from him by a considerable interval of time. Consequently "understanding" of Jesus was for John primarily an *historical knowledge*. How then does historical knowledge appear in John? This is intrinsically connected with the other question: How does he actually see Jesus, the hero of his history? The answer emerges from an analysis of his gnoseological terminology, the six terms: "to see", "to hear", "to come to know", "to know", "to testify", "to remember". We shall inquire what importance these terms have for a grasp of the Johannine mode of vision. Much work has already been done on these terms in detail and in partial studies, but not with the purpose of attaining by them a fundamental grasp of the Johannine mode of vision[1] and of answering the question, which Christ is really speaking in the Gospel according to John.

1. *"To see"* (ὁρᾶν, θεωρεῖν, θεᾶσθαι, βλέπειν)

In a study of the Johannine mode of vision a special place is naturally occupied by the word-group ὁρᾶν, θεωρεῖν, θεᾶσθαι, βλέπειν, all the more so because these words in fact play an important role with John. The verb θεᾶσθαι occurs in John (omitting the Apocalypse) 9 times (6 times in the gospel, 3 times in 1 John); θεωρεῖν 25 times (24 times in the gospel, once in 1 John); ὁρᾶν 39 times (31 times in the gospel, 8 times in 1 and 3 John); βλέπειν 18 times (17 times in the gospel, once in 2 John). In all, the four words for "seeing" are found 81 times. There seems to be no difference of meaning between them. This frequent occurrence of the verbs of seeing indicates immediately and clearly that the act of sight plays an important part in the Johannine process of knowledge. What is its significance there? This question is to be answered with the help of some texts from the Gospel according to John and the First Letter of John.

A particularly important text is found immediately in the prologue (1 : 14): "And the Word became flesh . . . and we have beheld (ἐθεασάμεθα) his glory, glory as of the only Son from the Father . . .". According to Bultmann "the theme of the gospel" finds expression here[2] because of course what is in question is: How can the divine glory be "visible" in the σὰρξ γενόμενος? The verb ἐθεασάμεθα (notice the aorist tense) primarily means being an historical eye-witness, and by the plural the author of the fourth gospel deliberately places himself in the "We"-circle of apostolic eye-witnesses of the life of Jesus.[3] This last itself indicates that this "communal" sight of the glory of the Logos in the incarnate must be more than a neutral observation of an historical fact, for in the latter sense the Jews too were eye-witnesses and yet did not see (cf. 9:39–41). With the apostolic eye-witnesses the *"seeing"* in contrast to that of the Jews was a seeing by faith; by no other faith, however, than the faith attested in the community of the apostolic Church. H. von Campenhausen has termed the plural ἐθεασάμεθα as a *pluralis ecclesiasticus,*[4] and in that way pointed to a factor that Bultmann too regards as operative in this seeing: the factor of the tradition in which the fourth evangelist knows he is placed. Bultmann remarks, "The seeing cannot be separated from this tradition" (cf. below VI, 2).

What was "seen" in the past is attested kerygmatically in the present: "And we have seen (perfect tense τεθεάμεθα) and testify (present tense μαρτυροῦμεν) that the Father has sent the Son as Saviour of the world" (1 Jn 4:14); at the same time, however, that is the traditional Christological doctrine of the Church even if the formulation is specifically Johannine. "The Father has sent the Son as Saviour of the world" is a statement of faith; the mission as such could not be observed. Yet 1 John says, "We have *seen* (this)". In reality the apostolic eye-witnesses saw the divinely-sent Saviour in the figure of Jesus of Nazareth, that is, in the form of an historical person. It is faith which in Jesus's coming "sees" the sending of the Saviour of the world. How did this believing "sight" come about, however? Certainly not by a process of logical inference: because Jesus of Nazareth did and said this and that, sat down to table with publicans and sinners, etc., "therefore" he must be the God-sent Saviour of the world. The act of seeing and the act of believing cannot in fact be separated from one another. By the fact that the apostle sees, he believes, and because he believes he "sees", namely the glory of the Logos and Son of God in the incarnate Jesus of Nazareth. "Only if the seeing which opens out faith is penetrated by faith, will the radiant power of God appearing be disclosed in Jesus's deeds" (H. Schlier).[5]

If 1 John can use the formula "we have seen and testify that God has sent the Son as Saviour of the world", this shows that here the act of sight has been and can be directly transposed into attested kerygma. The act of sight as such leads to attested kerygma, gives birth to it. In other words, what is seen becomes an attested kerygma which is handed on in the Church as a normative tradition. The θεάσασθαι "has turned the disciples into 'witnesses'" (A. Schlatter). What is the nature of this believing "sight" which leads to kerygma? As Bultmann rightly emphasized, it is "not a 'spiritual' seeing in the sense of the Greek contemplation of the Ideas or mysticism". The believing act of sight remains of course radically linked to the σὰρξ γενόμενος. In this "seeing" the "gaze is fixed on what is shown to it" (Schlatter). But what is shown? According to John 1 : 14, the δόξα of the Son. This shows itself concretely in what Jesus does. The disciples, for example, see what Jesus does at the marriage-feast at Cana, and at the same time they "see" in this action a revelation of his glory and so come to believe in him (cf. 2:11). The wording in 2:11: ἐφανέρωσεν τὴν δόξαν αὐτοῦ points out the right track: Jesus's concrete action is an epiphany of the Logos and Son.[6] In the historical actions of Jesus, and especially in his "signs", therefore, his divine glory is disclosed, although this remains almost completely hidden under the form of the incarnate Word and does not lead to continual "transfigurations" of his earthly mode of appearance. "This seeing of faith involves permitting oneself to be directed from the outer reality of Jesus's deeds to what they disclose by concealing: the might of the appearance of Jesus which gives light and life to all things, his *doxa* or glory. . . If the seeing consents to follow obediently what the sign points to, then the reality indicated in the sign opens itself to him as a gift" (Schlier).[7]

Particularly important for our purpose is 1 John 1–3. Reference is made four times in this difficult text[8] to the eye-witnesses' "historical" act of seeing (ἑωράκαμεν in v. 1; ἐθεασάμεθα, *ibid.*; ἑωράκαμεν in v. 2 and once again ἑωράκαμεν in v. 3). The eye-witnesses' act of seeing is focussed on "the word of life", "which was with the Father and appeared", and this means no other than Jesus Christ the Logos who has appeared in the flesh. How historical and real the meaning of this "seeing" is, is made sufficiently clear by the clause in verse 1 "and what our hands have touched". Linked with the perfect tense of ἑωράκαμεν, the verbs μαρτυροῦμεν and ἀπαγγέλλομεν in verses 2 and 3 are in the present tense. The testifying and announcing take place now, in the era of the Church; the "seeing" was an action in the past. What is attested and proclaimed in the era of the Church is "what" (ὅ) the eye-witnesses once "saw". They "saw" Jesus Christ, but once again not as a merely contingent historical fact, but as the Logos of life who "appeared"; once again the idea of epiphany enters into play in the term φανεροῦσθαι which twice occurs.

What do the apostolic eye-witnesses attest and announce in the Church and to the Church? Jesus as the redeemer who has appeared in the flesh. Not, therefore, Jesus in his historicity pure and simple nor as a purely heavenly redeemer, but *Jesus* as the bringer of salvation who has appeared in the world; and anyone who with faith accepts this kerygma "is of God" (4:2). The heretic on the contrary denies that Jesus is the Christ (cf. 2:22). The eye-witnesses' sight here too is once again not directed to Jesus as a merely historical figure. When they "saw" Jesus, in one and the same act they saw in him the bringer of salvation, the λόγος τῆς ζωῆς. That was possible because the historical Jesus is the epiphany of the eternal divine Logos. The act of sight, therefore, transcends what is on the surface, the temporal and historical, and penetrates to the mystery of this figure. But history and mystery do not thereby become contraries which exclude one another; the mystery reveals itself in history, that is, concretely, in Jesus of Nazareth. The act of sight opens out the historical figure for the kerygma which is to attest it.[9] In the kerygma the mystery of Jesus as an historical figure finds expression— literally so, for it is formulated in the kerygma, audibly expressed in it for the Church.

Who is it that actually speaks there? For the moment this question is only propounded; the answer will come later.

The Jews too "see" Jesus and his signs (cf. 2:23; 6:2), but the Johannine Christ puts the objection to them: "You have seen me and yet do not believe" (6:36) and his judgment consists, according to 9:39, precisely in the fact that those who do not see come to see and those who do see (like the Pharisees) become blind. Even if, therefore, John does use his four words for "seeing" equivalently, there are nevertheless decisive differences, not indeed in terminology, but in the act of seeing: the unbelievers see and yet do not "see"; believers on the contrary "see" behind the earthly appearance the mystery which is manifested.

It seems important to observe that John uses the term "seeing" in the sense we have just expounded, only in contexts which deal with the Jesus of history. He never calls the belief of the Christian community simply "sight". That shows clearly that for him the act of seeing cannot be understood in a purely intellectual or spiritual sense but remains inseparably connected with real physical sight such as is reserved to eye-witnesses. The community, on the other hand, is clearly told, "Blessed are those who have not seen and yet believe" (20:29).[10] If, therefore, through the act of seeing the historical figure of Jesus is opened out for the kerygma, that does not mean that in John's view believing and seeing are identical. The situation of the believing community is not, for John, the same as that of eye-witnesses who actually see; but the faith of the community has its historical origin in the believing sight of the eye-witnesses. The Church in the kerygma of faith receives the Christ whom the apostolic eye-witnesses have beheld, and so he also becomes the Christ who is preached, without ceasing on that account to remain Jesus. The Johannine Christ is not the product of the Church community's act of vision.

Already a first answer can be given to our fundamental question; how in general does John see his subject? He "sees" him in the way the eye-witnesses saw him and therefore with the eyes of faith; and that means, he sees him as the Logos and Saviour of the world who has appeared in the flesh.

2. *"To hear"* (ἀκούειν)

In the "act of seeing" it is not merely a question of sight in the actual, literal sense but of a more comprehensive process, to the complete constitution of which "hearing" too belongs, especially as hearing by general consent is the physical and intellectual organ of man through which to a quite decisive extent knowledge is achieved. This is particularly so in regard to religion, as not only the Johannine writings but the whole history of biblical revelation, especially the Old Testament itself, make us aware. That is essentially connected with the fact that revelation frequently occurred in words and as words intended to be "heard" by men.[11]

In the first place the philosopher must make his contribution, for he has important things to say on the phenomenology of hearing. "Listening to . . . is the intrinsically constitutive openness of the human being, as a social being, for others. Hearing even constitutes the primordial and specific openness of the human being for his own most personal active capacity for being, as hearing the voice of the friend whom each human being bears with him. The human being hears because he projectively and interpretatively understands. . . Listening to one another, by which mutual presence develops, has the possible modes of following and accompanying, and the privative modes of not hearing, opposing, defying and turning aside" (M. Heidegger).[12] This last sentence of the philosopher is confirmed by John's gospel. The allegories of the shepherd in chapter 10 clearly express the connection of hearing, knowing and following. "The sheep hear his voice" (10 : 3);[13]

"The sheep follow him for they know his voice" (10:4); "I am the good shepherd and I know my own and my own know me as the Father knows me and I know the Father" (10:14); "My sheep hear my voice and I know them and they follow me" (10:27). Thus being together and discipleship take shape in "hearing" which is founded on knowledge of others. The hearing is a consequence of this knowing and leads at the same time to even deeper knowledge, to γινώσκειν in the Johannine sense. According to Schlier, this hearing means "an attentive listening and concentration of attention in order to hear the voice or speech which comes forth", "a discriminating hearing", a "receptive and retentive hearing". For that reason such hearing is "the inner form of belief". "Hearing not only opens the way to faith but faith is accomplished in it."[14]

In precisely this way, therefore, the act of hearing with faith, which confers knowledge, makes possible the transposition of the words of Jesus directly heard by the apostolic witnesses, into the kerygma. And in the obedient acceptance of the kerygma their hearing is continued in the faithful hearing of the community. "What you heard from the beginning" (1 Jn 2:24, cf. 2:7; 3:11; 2 Jn 6) is the normative kerygma of the testimony of the apostolic hearers living on as apostolic tradition in the Church (cf. also 1 Jn 1:3). With John a line runs from the hearing of the Father by the Son via the hearing of the Son by the disciples to the hearing of the apostolic kerygma by the Christian community: "All that I have heard from the Father I have made known to you" (15:15); "What . . . we have heard we proclaim to you also" (1 Jn 1:3). The real mediator between the glorified Christ and those who announce his word in the Christian Church is, according to John 16:13, "the Spirit of truth": "Whatever he hears (from Christ in glory), he will declare". Thus Jesus's voice remains present and audible through the Paraclete in the apostolic kerygma, as part of which John's gospel itself in particular is to be reckoned. In it Christ himself makes himself heard, but through the medium of John's language in which the Johannine mode of vision created for itself the expression by which it can be heard.

3. *"To come to know"* (γινώσκειν : *to know, to recognize, to realize)*

Γινώσκειν is clearly a favourite word with John; it occurs in the gospel 56 times and 26 times in the letters (in Matthew 20 times, in Mark 12, in Luke 28, and 16 times in Acts). Moreover, with John the term very often has a markedly theological meaning on which a great deal has already been written.[15] What does it signify in connection with our theme of the Johannine mode of vision? In order to determine this, we may examine those texts in which the object of γινώσκειν takes the form of a ὅτι clause. In these ὅτι sentences "only Jesus appears as the object of the cognition and that in his quality as divinely-sent redeemer: that he is the saviour of the world (4:22), the Christ (7:26), that he is he (8:28), that he is in the Father and the Father is in him (10:38; 14:20), that he came from the Father (17:8), that the Father sent him (17:23, 25), that all he has is from the Father (17:7), that he loves the Father (14:31), that his teaching is from God

(7:17)" (A. Wikenhauser).[16] In short statements of a Christological kind are the object of the cognition in the ὅτι sentences.
It is repeatedly said in the fourth gospel that "the world"
or "the Jews" have not known Christ (1:10; 7:28 f.; 8:14,
19, 55; 9:29; 14:17; 15:21; 16:3; 17:25; cf. also 1 Jn 3:1);
the disciples on the other hand "know" him and precisely
because they are "not of the world", because they love, because
they have the *pneuma* of God and particularly because they
are believers. The πιστεύειν quite clearly tends with John
towards *knowing* (cf. Jn 6:69; 10:38; 14:9 ff.; 17:8; 1 Jn
4:16). Nevertheless there can "be no question . . . of complete
identity of the two terms" (Wikenhauser).

What actually happens when on the one hand Peter says to
Christ at 6:69, "We have believed and have come to know
that you are the Holy One of God", whilst on the other hand
the world has not recognized him? Clearly faith penetrates
the superficial, visible aspect of its object to which "the world"
remains attached. It perpetually overcomes by this penetration
the stumbling-block represented by the σὰρξ γενόμενος standing
before man as revealer "in sheer humanity" (Bultmann). In
faith, man acknowledges in the incarnate, the Logos, the
divine envoy, the Son of God. Faith, therefore, rises above the
superficial, visible aspect of the revealer and is receptive to his
mystery, and so from faith springs "knowledge" which leads
to a relation of a concrete and vital kind with the object of
faith, Jesus Christ. "If the verb γινώσκειν is used for this
relation, it does not mean a rational, theoretical knowledge
in which what is known confronts the knower with the
detachment of what is objectively perceived; but it means a
becoming aware, in which the knower is affected by what is

known . . . in his whole existence as a person" (Bultmann).[17] The believer in the act of knowing sees, of course, just as "the world" does, Jesus in his sheer humanity, but at the same time he sees made manifest in him the Logos and Son of God whom God has sent into the world. It would be a misconception to describe this process of coming to know as its object's "becoming transparent", because, of course, the "sheer humanity" of the revealer is not transfigured even for the believer and knower but is radically maintained. Nevertheless this believing knowledge makes possible in the same way as believing sight does, the transposition of the σὰρξ γενόμενος and his work and words, into the kerygma, the contents of which, with John, coincide with the objects of believing knowledge. The object of knowledge and the content of the kerygma in this way become and are identical. This makes possible the merging of the time-perspectives. For the kerygma puts forward for the present of the Church the contents of what came to be known in the past. Among the objects of the disciples' "knowledge" which are expressed in ὅτι clauses there belongs for example, according to the actual words of the Johannine Christ, his sending by the Father; compare 17:25, "And these have come to know that (ὅτι) thou hast sent me". In a kerygmatic formulation, the content of this ὅτι clause is also found in 3:34a ("He whom God has sent . . .") within a text (3:31–36) which, according to R. Schnackenburg, represented perhaps, originally, a portion of a homily of the evangelist.[18] That it is a matter here of a typical theme of Johannine preaching is shown by a comparison with 3:17 and 1 John 4:9, 10, 14, where in each case the sending of Jesus is part of the content of the kerygma.

This kerygma is therefore a "product" of the disciples' act of cognition. In other words, the "knowing" of Jesus (objective genitive) leads to the kerygma; the kerygma emanates from it into the domain of the Church. For of course, as we see from 1 John, John understands the kerygma explicitly as ecclesiastical kerygma. And so the "knowing" remains preserved from a false gnosis emancipated from the Church.[19]

Now it is important to observe that for John the process of believing "knowledge" is not limited to the time of the Jesus of history. He twice speaks in his gospel of a coming knowledge of the disciples. At 13:7 Jesus says to Peter, "What I am doing you do not know now, but after this ($\mu\epsilon\tau\grave{\alpha}$ $\tau\alpha\hat{\upsilon}\tau\alpha$) you will understand ($\gamma\nu\acute{\omega}\sigma\eta$)". What is actually meant by $\mu\epsilon\tau\grave{\alpha}$ $\tau\alpha\hat{\upsilon}\tau\alpha$ here? Commentators are agreed that it cannot refer to the explanation which Jesus gives the disciples at 13:12 ff.[20] A deeper insight is meant which will be conferred on them only after Jesus's glorification—an idea which is also found elsewhere in John's gospel (see below). Bultmann very pertinently remarks that $\mu\epsilon\tau\grave{\alpha}$ $\tau\alpha\hat{\upsilon}\tau\alpha$ refers "to the decisive turning-point which at this very moment is imminent, Jesus's death and resurrection". But what exactly is it that Peter will later "come to realize"? The fact that "his whole life was a service and self-sacrifice" (Wikenhauser), or, rather, that his going to his Passion and death for his own was "already comprised from the start in his coming" (Bultmann). Jesus's mission is a mission into death, "for the life of the world" (6:51c).[21] Peter will "come to know" that $\mu\epsilon\tau\grave{\alpha}$ $\tau\alpha\hat{\upsilon}\tau\alpha$, that is, what the faith of the Church is then proclaiming in the kerygma about the death of Jesus as a saving event and what the fourth evangelist himself makes the Baptist proclaim at

1 : 29 : " Behold the Lamb of God who takes away the sin of the world".[22] The "future" understanding thus leads once again to the kerygma.

The second text comes in the first farewell discourse (13 : 31—14 : 31) : "In that day you will know that I am in my Father and you in me and I in you" (14 : 20). "That day" is, in the context, the day on which Jesus "comes" (cf. v. 18) to his own, and by this "coming" very probably his coming in the Paraclete is meant (cf. v. 16).[23] What will the disciples come to know on that day? The mystery of the relation that links the Father, Jesus and those who are his. It is only to the post-paschal knowledge of faith, therefore, that the dimensions of the relation Father—Jesus—community, their mysterious mutual relationship, are manifested. And thereby at the same time the mystery of Jesus is known. For it is only correctly known on the basis of the relations in which Jesus stands. As a sharer in that knowledge, the evangelist expresses it in his gospel—and he does so in the literal sense : he formulates the mystery for the believing Church.

What is the nature of this knowledge? What is its relation to believing and seeing? It would probably be correct to say that this knowing, for John, expresses a believing sight and belief which sees, and gives it verbal utterance. In this way "knowing" also becomes a linguistic occurrence. The disciples see, for example, what Jesus does at the marriage in Cana; through what they experience they come to believe (2 : 11); the seeing belief comes to realize who Jesus is who is standing before them. And again "understanding" is expressed for example in the Christological predicates of the gospel which testify to the Church's belief. This also throws new light on the use of the past tenses at 6:69: "We have believed (πεπιστεύκαμεν) and have come to know (ἐγνώκαμεν) that you are the Holy One of God". These perfect tenses express the duration of the confession of faith and so deliberately carry it beyond the limits of the historical situation,[24] that is to say, the confession of faith is at the same time formulated as a confession of the faith of the Church in the special relation in which Jesus stands to the Father ("*the* Holy One of God"). 1 John 4:16 shows in addition that this profession of faith is expressed in typically Johannine language, for here the same perfect tenses πεπιστεύκαμεν and ἐγνώκαμεν occur, but in reverse order. Once again in John 6:69, therefore, the time perspectives merge; this process takes place even more strongly in "knowing" than in "seeing".

The perfect tense ἔγνωκαν is also found at 17:7 in a text which is of great importance for our purpose, for it again confirms what has just been said. "I manifested (ἐφανέρωσα) thy name to the men whom thou gavest me out of the world. Thine they were and thou gavest them to me and they have kept thy word (τετήρηκαν). Now they know (νῦν ἔγνωκαν) that everything that thou gavest me is from thee. For the words which thou gavest me, I have given to them (δέδωκα) and they received them (ἔλαβον) and they have come to know in truth (ἔγνωσαν ἀληθῶς) that I came from thee and believed (ἐπίστευσαν) that thou didst send me" (17:6-8). Here we have a connected group of terms (φανεροῦν-τὸν λόγον τηρεῖν-γινώσκειν-τα ῥήματα διδόναι-λαμβάνειν-πιστεύειν), which denote definite steps in the process of revelation. As origin the Father is named ("the words which thou gavest me"); his envoy Jesus Christ "makes known his name" and hands on the

words of the Father to the disciples; these in their turn keep
the word of the Father entrusted to them which they have
received from God's envoy and so come to "know" and
"believe". And they know "now" and "in truth" Jesus's
divine mission. But does this not involve a certain inconsistency
with Jesus's question at 16:31: "Do you now believe?"
W. Thüsing is therefore right in asking:[25] "Does 17:8 therefore perhaps not hold good of them?" His answer is: "Yes,
it does, but this faith which they have prior to the sending of
the Spirit is only the 'seed' of what shines through the saying
at 17:8 as the evangelist has shaped it. The evangelist already
sees through this inchoate faith . . . what the Spirit will later
effect in these men . . ." The "true (real) knowledge" will
come in the age of the *Pneuma*, who guides into the fullness
of truth. It is from this age that the evangelist formulates the
sentences at 17:6-8; the statements in the past tenses
τετήρηκαν, ἔγνωκαν, ἔλαβον, ἔγνωσαν (ἀληθῶς), ἐπίστευσαν are
spoken from the "now" of the age of the Church when the still
hesitant, uncertain faith, perpetually subject to temptations,
of the time before Easter, had long since become that firm
assurance of faith and "real" knowledge which is comprised
in the Johannine kerygma. What was once the particular
historical situation of the moment of farewell is opened out
and becomes the lasting situation of the age of the kerygma
in which the word is kept. It is the apostolic Church itself
which keeps this word which is the word of the Father and
of Jesus. In this way the line is apparent which leads from
the origin (the Father) through the envoy (Jesus) and the
apostles to the Church's kerygma, formulated in Johannine
language.

So it is precisely in John's gnoseological term "to know" or "to come to know" that the time perspectives merge and the hermeneutical situation of the fourth evangelist is apparent.

4. *"To know"* (εἰδέναι)

This gnoseological term is also met with very frequently in John, 85 times in the gospel (Matthew 25, Mark 22 and Luke 25 times) as well as 16 times in the letters. It is very close in meaning to γινώσκειν and is interchangeable with it[26] (cf. Jn 7:27 f.; 8:55 [cf. 8:19]; 13:7; 14:7; 1 Jn 2:21 [cf. 2 Jn 1]). It is possible, however, that in εἰδέναι the element of certainty is even more strongly implied than with γινώσκειν. In what follows we again choose statements which are of particular importance for our purpose.

The "world" or its representatives "the Jews" know neither the Father nor his envoy (cf. 1:26; 7:28; 8:14, 19, 54 f.; 9:29 f.; 15:21, etc.). At 14:5, however, Thomas says in the name of the disciples, "Lord we do not *know* where you are going; how can we *know* the way?" Wikenhauser remarks on this: "His objection is foolish; for he must have known long since that the way leads to the Father. But he is still labouring under the same error as the Jews (7:35 f.; 8:22) and Peter (13:37)". The "eye" of the disciples is not yet fully opened because their faith that Jesus is in the Father and the Father is in him is not yet firmly established and clarified (cf. 14:7-11). For that Thomas still needs another divine help.

According to 16:17 f. Jesus's revelation discourse to the disciples remains enigmatic and obscure: "What does that

mean? . . . We do not *know* (understand) what he says."
But through "seeing" Jesus again (cf. 16:22) "their lack of
understanding of Jesus's declarations, shown by their questions
will . . . have an end. The enigmatic obscurity which
previously enveloped his person and preaching . . . will then
have given place to complete clarity" (Wikenhauser). "In that
day you will not ask me any more questions" (16:23). The
phrase "in that day" is already found at 14:20;[27] there can
be no further doubt that what is meant is the day of the giving
of the Spirit (cf. 14:16) through which the mystery of Jesus
is disclosed to the disciples (and the Church). When they say
at 16:30: "Now we know that you know all things . . . by
this we believe that you came from God", this νῦν already
points to the age of the Pneuma, and the believing knowledge
"now" is already the knowledge of faith which "that day"
of the gift of the Spirit will confer and has already conferred
on the Church.

1 John 2:20 confirms this. "But you have anointing
(χρῖσμα) from the Holy One and you all know (οἴδατε)."
The "anointing" means the Holy Spirit whom the Christians
have received at baptism, and the "Holy One" very probably
refers to Christ as conferring the gift of the Spirit. The
possession of the gift of the Spirit has as its consequence that
"all"[28] orthodox believers "know". From the following verse
21 we learn what the object of the "knowledge" of believers
is: "the truth" as the "all-inclusive sum of what the 'Spirit
of truth' teaches" (Jn 16:13) (Schnackenburg), and there
belongs to it, above all, all knowledge of a Christological kind
(cf. merely the text which immediately follows 1 Jn 2:22 ff.).[29]
In the light of the statements of the First Letter of John, it is

clear that the "now" spoken of at John 16:30 is in fact the "now" of the era of the Pneuma in which true gnosis of Christ is given to the Church. The evangelist shares in it and states out of his own "knowledge" the goal to which the disciples were led through the "unction" of the Pneuma. Section V of the present essay (" The Johannine Mode of Vision and the Paraclete") will further confirm this.

The retrospective "knowledge" is found in a particularly remarkable way at the end of the First Letter: "We know (οἴδαμεν), however, that the Son of God has come and has given us understanding (διάνοιαν) so that we may come to know him who is true" (5:20). It is a question of the certain knowledge of faith about the theophany of the Son of God which has already taken place in Jesus Christ (ἥκει), and what Christ has given to the Church (ἡμῖν) is διάνοια, that is to say, knowledge and the faculty of knowing in one,[30] which here relates to the Father revealed by Jesus (= ἀληθινός). The Johannine Christ uses exactly the same term (ἥκειν) at 8:42 of his coming into the world which had already taken place; that is to say, he speaks in the language of the Johannine kerygma which is itself a fruit of the διάνοια given by Christ to the Church through the Spirit.

Thus the time-perspectives perpetually merge. *Comprehension* occurs and the fourth gospel was actually projected on the basis of this.

5. " To testify" (μαρτυρεῖν)

The terms "testify" (μαρτυρεῖν) and "testimony" (μαρτυρία)

occur very frequently in John: μαρτυρεῖν 33 times in the gospel, 10 times in the letters (Matthew once, Luke once); μαρτυρία 14 times in the gospel, 7 times in the letters (Mark 3 times, Luke once).[31] Testimony is given publicly. A witness usually appears in a law-suit and openly affirms what he has seen and heard. This public testimony by the witness has in itself a binding character. Examination of John's gospel confirms the correctness of this analysis which has in fact been drawn from it.[32] Thus the Baptist "testifies" publicly to Israel what he has "seen" (at Jesus's baptism), namely that "this is the Son of God" (Jn 1:34); he bears witness by this testimony to that most profound mystery of Jesus expressed in the Christological predicate "the Son". He bore witness "to the truth" (5:33). Jesus the incarnate Logos similarly "bears witness" to what he has "seen" (cf. 3:11), namely, in his pre-existence with the Father who bears witness to him (5:32, 37). Jesus also bears witness to himself and links with this the testimony of the Father who has sent him (8:18). His "works" also (which certainly do not only mean the "signs") bear witness to Jesus (5:36; 10:35), and so do the Old Testament scriptures (5:39).

The evangelist himself is a reliable witness for what he has written in his gospel (21:24; cf. also 19:35) and the circle of his disciples who publish his work "know" "that his testimony is true" (21:24b). The meaning of this remark in verse 24, according to Bultmann, is that "because the community knows that the testimony of that beloved disciple whom the 'brethren' according to verse 23 know to be a witness of the oldest generation, is always true, therefore the readers of the gospel will accept as true this testimony which he has expressed in the gospel". In that way the fourth gospel is understood by John's school itself as "testimony" to Christ, written by somebody who was in a position to give it—the present participle ὁ μαρτυρῶν in verse 24 ("who is bearing witness") is not intended to mean that the witness is still alive, but that his testimony has "not fallen silent with his death" (Bultmann). His testimony is not only an historical document intended to attest only past history, but is written in order to awaken faith "that Jesus *is* the Christ, the Son of God" (20:31) and that therefore the historical figure to whom witness is borne in the gospel is not a mere figure of the past but most present and living so that all who believe have life "in his name".

If the gospel is testimony which is also intended to awaken faith in what it testifies, this very fact expresses in principle the actualizing function of the testimony. Even though the author of the gospel is dead, his testimony lives on and in it that witness to the Father who is not dead, Jesus Christ. In this way the testimony of the gospel transcends the time and place of the historical Jesus and yet does not cease to be his testimony. The process of bearing witness goes on. But who actualizes the testimony? An answer is given at John 15:26 f. "The Spirit of truth . . . will bear witness to me; and you are also witnesses because you are with me from the beginning." The Spirit perpetually renders present in the Church the Christ-event and Christ's testimony. "The Spirit is the ground and cause, the 'principle' of the Johannine theology of re-presentation" (Blank).[33] His actual mode of operation remains to be examined in more detail (cf. Section V). With the testimony of the Spirit is linked that of the disciples—this link is verbally expressed by the co-ordinating conjunction καί, which joins the two sentences. The disciples are competent to bear such witness "because you are with me from the beginning", that is to say, because they are eye-witnesses and direct hearers of the historical Jesus, which also means that their testimony is not arbitrary in scope but is determined by what they have seen and heard (cf. 1 Jn 1:1); seeing and hearing are inseparably bound up with belief, understanding and knowledge, so that they are qualified in a quite definite way. The testimony of the disciples is something quite different from an historical report of Jesus's words and works in the presence of the public but it is an interpretative repetition of what Jesus revealed, and in this "interpretative understanding" the Spirit is also at work. Their testimony and that of the Spirit are identical in content. Its object is the mystery of Jesus (περὶ ἐμοῦ).

Once again the First Letter of John confirms what has been said. What the disciples "saw and attest and proclaim" is "the eternal life which was with the Father and was made manifest" (cf. 1 Jn 1:2), i.e., the incarnate Logos. That he is "the eternal life" could not be simply read off from him but could only be "seen" if one had come to believe. And what was "seen" in faith is the object of the later testimony and proclamation, not what is empirically verifiable. The object of testimony is therefore, of course, not an incidental characteristic or "aspect" of Jesus of Nazareth; it is not attested that he is *also* "Son of God", etc., but that he *is* the Messiah and Son of God (Jn 20:31), "true God and eternal life" (1 Jn 5:20). The object of the testimony is at the same time the object of the profession of faith; this emerges with all clarity from the First Letter of John (cf. for example 4:15; 5:5, 9–12). The content of the public testimony is the Christological truth.

The connection between historical eye-witness and representative testimony stands out particularly clearly from 1 John 4:14: "And we have seen (τεθεάμεθα) and testify (μαρτυροῦμεν) that the Father has sent the Son as Saviour of the world". The direct eye-witness refers to the past (perfect tense τεθεάμεθα), the testimony to the present (present tense μαρτυροῦμεν). "As τεθεάμεθα can hardly be conceived without an object, we must consider this as formally consisting in the ὅτι clause; this, however, gives the content of the testimony" (Schnackenburg on the passage). Because the act of seeing is not one of logical inference but a global one, the object of the τεθεάμεθα is also to be regarded as contained in the ὅτι sentence, that is to say, in the whole saving action of the Son, the believing eye-witnesses "see" this "state of affairs": God has sent the Son as saviour of the world. This state of affairs, however, is kerygmatically formulated and coincides in this formulation with the content of the self-revelation of the Johannine Christ, to some extent word for word (cf. Jn 5:36, 38; 6:29, 57; 7:29; 8:42; 17:3, 8, 21, 23, 25; and in addition 1 Jn 4:9 f.). The kerygma in which the testimony receives its formulation coincides verbally to a considerable extent with the revelation discourse of the Johannine Christ. The concrete Johannine testimony renders possible in this way the merging of the time perspectives, by which the revelation becomes an interpretatively comprehended revelation, without the past (the Jesus of history) becoming unimportant on that account.

6. *"To remember"* (*to bring to remembrance*) (μιμνῄσκεσθαι, μνημονεύειν, ὑπομιμνῄσκειν)

Though the words connected with remembering in the fourth gospel play a relatively small part statistically (μιμνῄσκεσθα 3 times; μνημονεύειν twice; ὑπομιμνῄσκειν once), the "theology" bound up with them is all the more important precisely for our present questions, as the following analyses will show.

The first important text is the Johannine description of the Cleansing of the Temple (Jn 2:13–22). The term μιμνῄσκεσθα occurs twice in it (vv. 17, 22). Verse 17 interrupts the account with the remark, "His disciples remembered (ἐμνήσθησαν) that it was written (Ps 68:10 LXX) 'zeal for thy house will consume me (καταφάγεται)'". The future tense καταφάγεται is certainly the original reading.[34] "John reads his words as a prophecy of the messianic action of Jesus" (Barrett),[35] but the "consume" does not mean the "inner fire" which fills Jesus as he drives the money-changers from the Temple.[36] "The evangelist is rather already envisaging what follows— the whole of Jesus's activity—and means that Jesus's zeal will bring him to death" (Bultmann); corresponding to this, at the end of the pericope in verse 22, is a reference to his resurrection. Precisely on account of the "total unified view" of the life of Jesus which is apparent here, it is extremely probable that the ἐμνήσθησαν, even in verse 17, already refers to the postpaschal "remembering" of the disciples[37] which brings with it a deeper Christological understanding of scripture. Scripture opens out to the understanding of the disciples and the Church in the light of what had happened.

That becomes particularly clear in verse 22. "When therefore he was raised from the dead, his disciples remembered (ἐμνήσθησαν) that he had said this; and they believed the scripture and the word that Jesus had spoken." The observation in the text "when he was raised from the dead" not only serves to indicate the time but also states the reason that made it possible for the disciples to remember in such a way that belief was linked with it. It was the raising of Jesus from the dead which made possible the believing remembrance in which understanding unfolds. Remembrance first of all re-presents a saying of Jesus which he had uttered in his prepaschal life, but his words are not only reproduced by memory but at the same time are unfolded for faith. In the actual context of the pericope, this means that the disciples realize in their remembrance that Jesus's spiritual resurrected body is the "temple"[38] of the eschatological era of salvation in which the promise of scripture about a new temple has already mysteriously been fulfilled: the risen Christ takes the place of the old temple.[39] Consequently the remark of the gospel at verse 21, "but he said this in regard to the temple which is his body"[40] is an explanatory remark of the evangelist in the light of the postpaschal remembrance which gave both faith and understanding. And therefore the content of the remembrance in verse 22 expressed as a brief ὅτι clause (ὅτι τοῦτο ἔλεγεν) does not refer back to the ἔλεγεν of verse 21 but to the enigmatic statement of Jesus in verse 19, "Destroy this temple and in three days I will raise it up", which he deliberately leaves obscure for the Jews; for he gives no answer to their question in verse 20. In other words, the prepaschal history of Jesus only exhibits to the believing understanding of the Church its actual revelation content in the postpaschal

41

anamnesis. The anamnesis makes possible the transposition of history into kerygma and to this there also essentially belongs the κατὰ τὰς γραφάς, that is to say, a new, Christological understanding of the scriptures. It is therefore permissible to say, providing it is correctly understood, that Jesus's resurrection is operative even in the kerygma, in which the "letter" of scripture becomes "spirit" and scripture discloses its Christological dimensions. In the believing remembrance which Jesus's resurrection from the dead involves for the disciples and the Church, the life of Jesus becomes kerygmatically transparent and unfolds into the gospel.

The term "to remember" occurs again in a similarly important sense at 12:16. "His disciples did not understand (ἔγνωσαν) this at first (τὸ πρῶτον) but when Jesus was glorified they remembered (τότε ἐμνήσθησαν) that this had been written of him and had been done to him." The sentence has five parts, and all are important for our purpose: a) the temporary lack of understanding by the disciples b) Jesus's glorification in his resurrection c) the remembrance by the disciples which this made possible and which refers to two things (i) the Christological content of scripture and (ii) the historical circumstances of Jesus's entry into Jerusalem.

The pericope to which 12:16 belongs, tells of Jesus's entry into Jerusalem (12:12-19; cf. Mt 21:7-9; Mk 11:7-10; Lk 19:35-38). The pilgrims who had come up for the festival greet Jesus as they meet him with the cry, "Hosanna! Blessed is he who comes in the name of the Lord (Ps 118, [117] 25 f.), the King of Israel". In verse 14 an observation of the evangelist follows: "Jesus however found a young ass and sat upon it", and in addition, by way of comment, a quotation from

Zechariah 9:9 (linked with Is 40:9): "Fear not daughter of Zion; behold your king is coming sitting on an ass's colt!"

What did the disciples "at first" not "understand"? The answer follows from the ὅτι clause in verse 16 which once again mentions the contents of the disciples' remembrance. At first they do not understand that what historically occurred at Jesus's entry into Jerusalem is the fulfilment of the saying of a prophet, Zechariah. In that way they do not recognize either (or not yet clearly enough), that he is the coming king, i.e., the Messiah. Perhaps they had a vague notion of his messianic mystery before Easter. But they did not understand at first that Jesus's entry on an ass's colt implied a quite definite conception of the Messiah, because it was only Easter that opened their eyes to the Christological meaning of scripture. Remembrance renders present to them once more the historical scene at Jesus's entry into Jerusalem and in the light of Jesus's glorification in his resurrection[41] there awakens at the same time the remembrance of the words of the prophet at Zechariah 9:9, in which of course the coming king of Zion is seen "riding on an ass", "the mount of the ordinary man and peaceable citizen at all periods" (Nötscher on the passage), who will bring a rule of peace, "Lo, your king comes to you; just and victorious is he, humble and riding on an ass, on a colt, the foal of an ass. He destroys the chariots in Ephraim, the war-horses in Jerusalem. The battle bows are destroyed. He commands peace to the nations. His rule extends from sea to sea, from the river to the ends of the earth" (Zech 9:9 f.). The disciples only recognize "that this had been written of him" (Jn 12:16b) in the postpaschal "remembrance" which brought a new understanding of scripture with it.

In addition the disciples realized in this process of recollection "that this . . . had been done to him" (ὅτι . . . ταῦτα ἐποίησαν αὐτῷ). Probably the pilgrims are thought of as the subject to ἐποίησαν and what was done by them is their act of homage to Jesus on his entry into Jerusalem.[42] That means that even the deeper meaning of this unexpected homage of the crowd, which to a large extent took place in the words of scripture (cf. 12:13), only became clear to the disciples in their postpaschal remembrance. Now they recognized that the homage, though its import was not expressly known to the crowd, was paid to the messianic Saviour-king, Jesus Christ.

In principle we can say on the basis of the analyses just given of these two "remembrance" texts of the fourth gospel that the true meaning of Jesus's life before Easter, as regards both his words and the events of his life, disclosed itself to the disciples and so to the Church only after Jesus was glorified, that is to say, after his resurrection from the dead.[43] Two things were implied, in the mind of the fourth evangelist, by his conceiving this postpaschal knowledge of the life of Jesus as among other things a process of anamnesis. In the first place "remembrance" is directed to an historical event, to past history, in this case to the history of Jesus of Nazareth. Furthermore, it is directed to the hidden meaning of this history which is disclosed in a knowing and believing anamnesis and finds expression for the Church in the kerygma. The gospel understood in this way is an explanatory anamnesis of the life of Jesus. (This point is dealt with further in the Excursus, "The Gospel as anamnesis", p. 48 below.)

Who, however, made possible such explanatory recollection by the disciples? According to John 14:26, it is the Paraclete, sent by the glorified Christ, who brings to the remembrance of the disciples all that Jesus had said to them. This will be dealt with more closely in Section V.

7. Conclusion: the Johannine kerygma as the "product" of the Johannine act of vision

The Johannine mode of vision, or perspective, with which this *quaestio* is concerned, has been exhibited by an analysis of the gnoseological concepts of "seeing", "hearing", "coming to know", "knowing", "testifying" and "remembering" which constitute it. Since John's interest is directed to an historical subject-matter, the mode of vision of the fourth evangelist is at the same time what has been called "historical reason", which is concerned with the way in which an historian envisages his subject. The Johannine mode of vision is that of a believing and informed witness who, in remembrance, "sees" his subject, Jesus of Nazareth, in such a way that the latter's hidden mystery becomes "visible" and expressible for the Church in the kerygma. This act of vision is, therefore, a creative process. It renders possible the transposition of the knowledge obtained by it into the testimony of the kerygma. The latter is actually realized in the Church as anamnesis and in it Jesus continues to live and speak as glorified by the Paraclete. The Johannine kerygma, we may say, is the product of the Johannine mode of vision.

In the case of the fourth evangelist his act of vision has a long history. It started of course at the time when he was an eye-witness, when the apostolic circle ("We") accompanied

Jesus on his ways (cf. for example once again the past tense of
ἐθεασάμεθα at John 1:14). It only becomes clear, however,
"when Jesus was glorified", in other words, after his resurrection. And it attains its full nature in the Christological
tradition of the apostolic Church in which what was seen has
become the formulated kerygma. The "seeing" of the eye-
witnesses in this way becomes in "remembrance" the retrospective gaze of witnesses who come to realize and know. It
can never, however, become something entirely individual for
the "We"-circle lives in and as the community of the Church
(cf. the plural μαρτυροῦμεν).

In the act of vision the time-horizons merge, but this of
course must not be misunderstood. In this merging, the past
is not annulled; in its actualization for the present and in the
present, it entirely preserves its importance, supplying the
material by which the act of vision can perpetually enkindle
anew. But the act of vision takes its bearings not only from
the past, but also from the present, in this case from the
present time of composition with its questions. Precisely these
questions, the situation in theological history, contribute to
determining the direction of the act of vision; they provide the
angles from which the historical material (to which tradition
also belongs) is focussed. To put it concretely, Jesus of
Nazareth is so expressed by John in his act of vision that the
history of Christ projected and presented by him simultaneously gives an answer to the Christological questions of
the time of its composition. This answer is not, however,
obtained by speculation about the mystery of Jesus, but
precisely by that retrospective gaze which the act of vision
makes possible, as has been seen by analysis of the gnoseological

terms. Retrospection is not a mechanical reproduction of the history of Jesus, and in the act of vision there occurs the exposition effected by the Spirit, and so the historical Jesus becomes the Christ of the kerygma, who precisely as such is also the Jesus of history. For "history" in the proper sense is of course "history as operative influence".[44] The conscious position of the witness in the "We"-circle (of eye-witnesses, the Church and its tradition) prevents at the same time the kerygmatic Christ from becoming the Christ of a private gnosis as the Christ of the προάγων is (cf. also note 17, p. 106).

EXCURSUS. THE GOSPEL AS ANAMNESIS

We have seen (Section III, 6) that the gospel is an interpretative anamnesis of the life of Jesus. This was said with reference to John's gospel. But what applies in particular to this gospel holds good of the biblical writing of history generally. Scripture aims in principle at being anamnesis, *repraesentatio*, a "rendering present", because of course for the community to which it is read it possesses a contemporary relevance and function even though the degree of immediate application may be very different from book to book of the Bible.

1. The idea that the actualizing proclamation of past saving deeds of God in the community is "remembrance" is already found in the Old Testament.[1] The researches of Zirker in particular show that the essential elements of the anamnesis theology of the fourth gospel connected with the Johannine mode of vision are already found in the Old Testament tradition and viewpoint.[2] Thus in the Psalms the present representation in memory of Israel's past is frequently described as "seeing" Yahweh's sacred deeds. With the cry " 'Come and see what God has done' (66:5) the assembly for divine worship is summoned in the liturgy to contemplate redemptive history" (Zirker).[3] The past extends into the present if only in words.[4] In Psalm 46:9 also ("Come and see

the works of Yahweh"), the "beholding" is "the convinced perception of the saving reality present in the celebration" (Zirker).[5] Narrated past and narrating present are joined particularly clearly in Psalm 48:9: "As we have heard so we see in the city of the Lord of hosts . . ."; and in Psalm 40:4 we read, "many see and fear and put their trust in Yahweh": "This means, quite in accordance with the representation, that the proclamation of the past event (v. 2 ff.) which we hear in the 'new song' is at the same time a living experience of what is proclaimed" (Zirker).[6]

The "We"-style plays a large part in this also,[7] especially in the confessions of guilt, "Both we and our fathers have sinned" (Ps 106:6). "With all urgency the community is to experience the identity of the situation of their fathers with their own saving history" and so enter anew into the situation "in which they—in their fathers—had already once been summoned to decision" (Zirker).[8]

With this representation in dramatic language the time-interval is bridged.[9] Thus in Psalm 132, "in the memorial celebration" the community becomes "witness of David's endeavours to bring the ark of the covenant from Kiryathyearim to Jerusalem: 'Lo we heard of it in Ephrathah, we found it in the fields of Jaar' (v. 6)" (Zirker).[10] The community shares in experiencing in anamnesis what once happened to the forefathers. In this the narrative itself remains perfectly aware of the time-interval. Zirker rightly remarks, "Such duality of time is characteristic of the descriptive representation in these psalms which should not be interpreted as meaning that it is to liturgical worship as such that 'the suppression of historical distance' [Weiser] is to be attributed".[11] What links the ages is the "consciousness of the presence of God linking the ages into a unity".[12]

What is the relation here between the uniqueness of the historical fact and its meaning which is present in the liturgy? Zirker goes very thoroughly into this question[13] and what he has to say is of great importance for our theme of the Johannine perspective and the question of the Jesus of history. He stresses that the problem of liturgical anamnesis in the Bible cannot be reduced to the alternative of a present representation of the past or of a transporting of the community into the past. For the Israelite, liturgy was "always aware of the chronological sequence of the generations despite the urgency of the representation".[14] "The inner tension which springs from the character of historical times as past, is not suppressed but is precisely a ground of the present generation's obligation to take up the offer which was bestowed on the fathers to be handed on."[15] The " 'triple measure' of the time image" (Eichrodt)—past, present, future—is not suppressed; its unity makes possible the divine saving action. Zirker speaks of "mediated immediacy" as the closest relation to the past, "Mediated—for the interval is there to be bridged; immediacy —for in worship there is manifested a vital concern with what is already chronologically withdrawn from the present".[16] Precisely when it was no longer a question only of "festival themes" but of the growing together of different traditions of redemptive history, the awareness of the interval inevitably increased.[17] The "remembrance" deliberately stresses the time interval, and at the same time overcomes it. The $\dot{\epsilon}\phi'\dot{a}\pi a\xi$ of the event in sacred history is not lost in the remembrance but is rendered actual for the community.[18] In present commemoration the past saving action is not renewed but is represented in its enduring redemptive significance for the community. In remembrance the past saving deed becomes the community's "today" in which God himself renders the past present in the meaning and obligation it bears. "You stand this day all of you before Yahweh your God . . . , that you may enter into the sworn covenant of the Lord your God which Yahweh your God makes with you this day" (Deut 29: 10, 12). In this "today" there arises "the intrinsic analogy with the situation of the forefathers' decision" (Zirker). [19] The actualization is, therefore, not unlimited, and does not abolish the time-intervals. It is rather the case that "Encounter with the past in the liturgical representation is based on the 'narration' which depends on the interval between the generations and is also based on knowledge of the presence of the God of history; the fact that the reality of the historical events established long ago can now be vividly experienced in worship is not to be understood as though 'all spatial and temporal distance were lost' [Weiser]" (Zirker). [20]

2. These conclusions of Zirker's work also apply *mutatis mutandis* to John's gospel and his mode of vision. Actualizing anamnesis occurs here of course not in liturgy but through the inspired writer; liturgy takes over this task only secondarily when the gospel is read out to the congregation assembled for divine worship. By hearing his words, the community shares in the sacred writer's original "act of vision" which produces "knowledge"; [21] in the words of the gospel the Lord himself comes before them and speaks to them through the Paraclete and the latter through the evangelist. [22] His words and works are actualized in this, and in the case of John's

gospel to such a degree that it is no longer the "historical" Jesus who stands before the congregation but the glorified Christ. The latter, however, remains identical with the Jesus of history, even if not in his mode of being. This goes so far in the fourth gospel that the inspired mouthpiece of the glorified Christ, the sacred writer, lends him his tongue, so that Christ speaks to the Christian community in Johannine language. (On this cf. also Section VII.)

As it listens to his words, the congregation is taken into the "fellowship" (1 Jn 1 : 3) of the apostolic "We"-circle and shares in its knowledge and remembrance. The act of vision is to a certain extent multiplied and yet remains firmly linked to the apostolic "We"-circle and thereby to apostolic tradition and by this in turn to the Jesus of history (cf. 1 Jn 1 : 1-4).[23] In this way, however, the time-interval also is just as relevant as it is in the Old Testament conception of anamnesis, and retains its hermeneutical function of establishing "perspective".

John, therefore, is not alone in his conception that the writing of a gospel involves a process of anamnesis which renders the past present and produces knowledge. He stands wholly in a tradition reaching far back to the Old Testament era. To a limited extent there was precedent for this in the synoptic manner of composing gospels.

3. The synoptics also in fact understood their works in a certain sense as actualizing representation and anamnesis;[24] among them especially Luke, the "theologian of paradosis" (Schürmann). When he shows the apostle Paul addressing the admonition to the presbyters of Ephesus in his "farewell discourse" in Miletus always "to remember (μνημονεύειν) the words of the Lord Jesus" (Acts 20 : 35), that is meant to be a

pattern to follow. In the evangelical tradition the words of Jesus are presented "just as they were delivered . . . by those who from the beginning were eye-witnesses and ministers of the word" (Lk 1:2) and were transmitted in the catechetical λόγοι of baptismal instruction to the catechumens (1:4), so that for the Christian churches of the post-apostolic era the "remembrance" of his words is possible. In this "remembrance" the word of the historical Jesus is rendered present for the congregation. The gospel has a representative function. It "renders present the apostolic paradosis and causes it to speak directly in its spiritual power and beget faith" (Schürmann).[25] The "us" (cf. Lk 1:2—an ecclesiological "We"!) of the πράγματα πεπληροφορημένα (1:1) handed down by the apostolic eye-witnesses—the Christological redemptive facts— are "at all times 'close' to the generation of the eschatological era as given facts—ἐν ἡμῖν. As eschatological facts they retain their eschatological character as present, remaining always present to us in the Church" (Schürmann).[26] Luke gathers in his gospel the (pre-Lucan) "narratives" (διηγήσεις) of the apostolic period about Jesus in "such a valid and authoritative manner" that now his written gospel too can "represent the facts of redemption" just like the apostolic paradosis itself.[27] In this way the words and work of the historical Jesus become present at all times for the Church by way of the apostolic traditions and their transmission by the πολλοί narratives and Luke himself. This is a process which in the New Testament culminated and concluded in the fourth gospel.

The total bringing to remembrance which, according to Schlier,[28] is what John's gospel is, is distinguished, however, from the Lucan conception of the representative function of

53

scripture by the fact that the specific Johannine mode of vision is operative to such a high degree in the process of representative anamnesis, that thereby the actualization of Jesus's words and work took place and takes place for the Church in the words of this gospel in a quite unsurpassable way.

IV

KNOWLEDGE AND LOVE

In the Johannine act of vision another factor is operative which has not been taken into account in what has been said so far: the love of the disciple for his master.

Max Scheler in particular has drawn attention, by reference to St Augustine, to the connection between love and knowledge.[1] This link was known to John when he wrote in the First Letter (4:7): πᾶς ὁ ἀγαπῶν ... γινώσκει τὸν θεόν. In the following verse he gives as a reason the nature of God, "for God is love". "Love as such is the kind God is" (R. Schnackenburg),[2] and so those who love God come to know him in their love; they "know" of what kind God is, God's nature manifests itself to those who love him in their love, so that they become "clear-sighted" for God. Verse 9 goes on, "In this the love of God was made manifest among us, that God sent his only Son into the world . . ." God's love is not abstract; it expresses itself and dispossesses itself in the radical self-communication which the sending of the Son into the world involves. God's love reveals itself in a unique way in the sending of the Son, or more precisely in the one who is sent himself, and the loving believer comes to know God by experience when in Jesus Christ he has the Son before his eyes.[3] And so those who love recognize God himself in the incarnate Son. The loving gaze of the believer is directed to Jesus Christ and "recognizes" God in him; for "he who has seen me has seen the Father" (Jn 14:9). And so it is quite in accordance with the mind of John to interpret his sentence "He who loves, knows God" Christologically and to say, "He who loves, knows Jesus". It was on the basis of this experience that John wrote his history of Christ. Because he loved his subject, he could penetrate into the mystery of Jesus and give expression to it in the gospel. Love is what most renders possible "the perception of what is other" (M. Scheler).

His love, however, was a requited and invited love. According to John 21:20, 24, of course, the author of the fourth gospel is the disciple "whom Jesus loved", the so-called beloved disciple (cf. also 13:23; 19:26; 20:3; and also 1:40; 18:15 f.).[4] According to 21:20, he had the place of honour at the side of Jesus at the Last Supper; he could question Jesus and he received an answer. "The place at Jesus's side corresponds to the place of Jesus at the Father's side; just as this place makes him the revealer of the Father,[5] so the beloved disciple's place makes him Jesus's revealer and exegete" (W. Grundmann). This "exegesis" of Jesus constitutes the fourth gospel.

A. Kragerud would like to regard the beloved disciple as the exponent of a post-apostolic, "Johannine" type of prophecy, a personification of a circle of wandering prophets.[6] As a historical figure the beloved disciple, for Kragerud, is "purely and simply a fiction".[7] We should prefer to say with Grundmann, "the beloved disciple is both individual and type; if as an individual he dies, as type he endures".[8] In the fourth gospel the beloved disciple is placed in a quite special relation to Peter (cf. 21 : 15–23) in a way which almost shows a certain superiority of the beloved disciple over Peter. This "consists in the first place in the fact that the beloved disciple outlives him and becomes of an importance for the Church by which, at the conclusion of the apostolic age, its apostolic character is guaranteed and maintained. He is a witness of what he reports" (Grundmann). In addition he is a charismatic interpreter of Christ's history, and clearly knows that he is guided in this by the Paraclete. Schlier endeavours to express the matter as follows:[9] "The 'beloved disciple' is not indeed, according to John, the symbol of a group of prophets, but the thesis might well be maintained that as compared with Peter as the representative of the official ministry and in communion with him, he represents the charismatics." John 21 : 15–23 testifies to this "fellowship" between the beloved disciple and Peter; for it is of course Peter himself, according to verse 20, who turns round and sees the beloved disciple, and this turning and seeing is an expression of their association. Of rivalry between Peter and the beloved disciple as Kragerud views it,[10] there can, therefore, be no question. According to the fourth gospel itself, the promise of the Paraclete holds good of the whole college of apostles, not of a special charismatic circle.[11] The "We"-circle as it is expressed in such formulas as "we have seen", refers not to charismatic wandering prophets of the post-apostolic age but primarily to the apostolic witnesses who saw and heard Jesus in his lifetime, from whose preaching the apostolic tradition concerning Jesus derives. John also acknowledges this tradition (cf. Section VI on this), but nevertheless interprets it independently, giving special theological emphasis to this or that element and to a large extent clothing it in a language which is unmistakably his own. We do not think we are mistaken in placing the ultimate basis of the independent interpretation of Jesus's words and work in John's gospel in the unique relation in which the beloved disciple stood to Jesus. At the Last Supper he was nearest to Jesus and so, more than all the others who took part, could become his interpreter. What Max Scheler expresses as a general principle as follows, "The moral centre of the person of Jesus . . . is given to only one, his disciple. Only discipleship opens the door to this gift",[12] holds good in a special degree of the beloved disciple; the mystery of Jesus is open to him even more than to the others. Consequently his testimony has special rank. In it the love of the disciple for the master finds expression. As Jesus's beloved disciple who was called to love and allowed himself to be so called, he was particularly qualified to "see" and to "know" Jesus and to attest in the Church this knowledge[13] conferred by the ἀγάπη of Jesus.[14] Love was his charisma but this charisma did not set him in rivalry with the prior apostolic tradition of the Church concerning Jesus. For charisma (Spirit) and tradition do not need to be in opposition. The Spirit who is active in the charisma is also of course operative in tradition; the latter itself is his work.

V

THE JOHANNINE MODE OF VISION AND THE PARACLETE

Reference has already been made in previous chapters to the importance of the Pneuma and Paraclete for the Johannine mode of vision. This must now be examined systematically.[1] This can best be done by means of the verbs used to make statements about the "Spirit of truth" such as are found in the five Paraclete sayings in John's gospel (Jn 14:16 f.; 14:25 f.; 15:26; 16:7b–11; 16:12–15). They are as follows: εἶναι (μεθ'ὑμῶν, ἐν ὑμῖν), μένειν (παρ ὑμίν), διδάσκειν (cf. also 1 Jn 2:27), ὑπομιμνῄσκειν, μαρτυρεῖν, ἐλέγκειν (omitted from consideration here), ὁδηγεῖν, λαλεῖν, ἀναγγέλλειν, δοξάζειν. Some essential points have already been made regarding the terms ὑπομιμνῄσκειν and μαρτυρεῖν in Section III, but these must now be supplemented with regard to the Paraclete.

We start from the term διδάσκειν in the second Paraclete saying (14:26). διδάσκειν means literally "teach, instruct", but in John it nearly always means to reveal; cf. especially John 8:28 (χαθὼς ἐδίδαξεν με ὁ πατήρ, ταῦτα λαλῶ); 1 John 2:27 (. . . τὸ αὐτοῦ χρίσμα διδάσκει ὑμᾶς περὶ πάντων); the subject of the sentence χρίσμα is the Holy Spirit[2] who is viewed in closest union with Christ ([ὃ ἐλάβετε απ']αὐτοῦ= Christ as glorified); he "teaches" the Church "about everything" still, even now (present tense διδάσκει) as he already has taught them previously (καθὼς ἐδίδαξεν ὑμᾶς). The object "everything", about which the Spirit teaches the Church, appears from the context to refer particularly to Christology; in the Christological homologesis in which the Church holds fast to the apostolic tradition valid "from the beginning", the Spirit is at work (cf. 2:22–24). This "teaching" function of the Spirit is also spoken of in the second Paraclete saying (Jn 14:26), in a future tense, it is true (ἐκεῖνος ὑμᾶς διδάξει) because it is spoken from the situation of the farewell discourses and therefore in view of the glorification of Jesus which is still to come. Here too the content of the teaching is signified by πάντα. As verse 26 is a deliberate continuation (cf. the continuative particle δέ) of what Jesus is saying in verse 25 ("these things [ταῦτα] I have spoken to you while I am still with you"), πάντα refers back to the ταῦτα of verse 25, that is, to Jesus's words of revelation to his disciples during his prepaschal activity. Now according to the mind of the fourth gospel, the "Helper's" "teaching all things" certainly does not consist in serving as a mere prop to the memory of the disciples (and the Church) designed to prevent the words of revelation of the historical Jesus from fading from their minds, so to speak. The διδάσκειν just like the ὑπομιμνῄσκειν, which immediately follows, is a rendering present which at the same time implies interpretation; this follows from the whole tendency of the Paraclete sayings. Bultmann is surely right[3] in thinking that διδάσκειν and ὑπομιμνῄσκειν at John 14:26 form a unity:[4] the teaching is a bringing to remembrance and the remembrance is a teaching, and both signify, not the mechanical reconstruction and reproduction of past events and words, but the manifestation of their meaning for the Church. Precisely in the circumstance, however, that the object of this explanatory teaching and bringing to remembrance by the Paraclete is the revelation of the historical Jesus, the connection is evident between the Paraclete and Jesus, or even more plainly, the dependence of the former on Jesus. The Paraclete is not a figure parallel to Jesus who is to complete Jesus's revelation or even (as a rival) to replace it by a new and better one, but is the instrument of the glorified Christ, who preserves Jesus's words and work for the Church, renders them present and interprets them.[5] For that reason the words of Jesus which the Paraclete brings to the remembrance of the Church are his interpreted words.

Another important statement about the Paraclete is made in the third saying (15:26): ἐκεῖνος μαρτυρήσει περὶ ἐμοῦ. The term μαρτυρεῖν has already been dealt with in some detail (cf. III, 5). Testimony is given publicly before the world. "It is testimony which reveals and summons to faith and therefore seeks to convince, and is addressed to the world, or it is testimony which professes faith, rejects and judges unbelief . . ."(Blank).[6] Its essential content is Christ (περὶ ἐμοῦ). Once again the statement is made in the "style of promise" (future tense μαρτυρήσει), as spoken in the situation of the farewell discourses.

Where does the Paraclete bear witness to Christ? Not in private revelations but in the concrete official testimony of the apostolic eye-witnesses and hearers (15:27), whose testimony is not a past one but continues at the present time (present tense μαρτυρεῖτε), whose close association with Christ endures (present tense again ἐστε) and who can also be witnesses to the historical Jesus ($\dot{\alpha}\pi$' $\dot{\alpha}\rho\chi\hat{\eta}s$). In their testimony the testimony to Christ of the Spirit goes forth in the world;[7] this is clear from the co-ordinating $\kappa\alpha\acute{\iota}$ which links verses 26 and 27.

This co-ordination is also found in another text which is important for our purpose, at 1 John 5:6b, "and the Spirit bears witness". What does it attest? That Jesus is the Son of God who has come by water and blood (v. 6a). The Spirit, therefore, attests the unity of the eternal Christ who is preached with the historical, crucified Jesus of Nazareth (cf. also 1 Jn 4:2). Now this is the fundamental theme of apostolic Christology. But it is the glorified Christ who will send the Spirit of truth (Jn 15:26; 16:7), and he himself comes in him to the disciples (14:18); "In that day" they will "come to know that I am in my Father and you in me" (14:20). The Pneuma therefore attests for the Church the full reality of Christ; in the concrete apostolic testimony this finds expression for the Church. If according to the fifth Paraclete saying (16: 13-15), the Spirit "will take what is mine and declare it to you", because he "will not speak on his own authority but whatever he hears ($\dot{\alpha}\kappa o\acute{\upsilon}\epsilon\iota$) he will speak", then what is Jesus's is also what belongs to the glorified Christ on high and what is "heard" is his message. For the present tense $\dot{\alpha}\kappa o\acute{\upsilon}\epsilon\iota$ must be noticed;[8] the Spirit always "hears" what the one on high speaks, and transmits it to the Church.

What does the Spirit "hear"? Not mysterious things which are then transmitted to initiates (as the Gnostics in their works claimed) but the words of Jesus and the Father, for "all that the Father has is mine" (v. 15a). The words of Jesus and those of the Father cannot therefore be rigidly separated (cf. also

7:17 f.; 12:49; 14:10). "But that means precisely that the words of the Spirit are not new as compared with those of Jesus, but that the Spirit will only say the latter anew"; in the proclamation effected by the Spirit "Jesus's words continue to operate" (Bultmann on 16:13). "In the Church's preaching supported by the Spirit, Jesus's words continue to live and operate by being more deeply grasped, more abundantly unfolded and proclaimed in accordance with the needs of the particular situation" (Wikenhauser). In this way the Spirit will "guide" (ὁδηγήσει) the Church "into all truth". In the context (16:12) the Johannine Christ says, "I have yet many things to say to you but you cannot bear them now". When he continues, "When the Spirit of truth comes he will guide you into all the truth", it is clear from this that the fullness of truth into which the Spirit guides is the continuing word of Jesus, more precisely of the glorified Christ. The expression ἀλήθεια πᾶσα is "linked to Jesus, truth in person" (Thüsing).[9] Then the process which is denoted by ὁδηγεῖν is not something entirely new and independent taking place side by side with the proclamation of Jesus. What the disciples primarily cannot yet "bear" is, according to Thomas Aquinas (in his commentary on this passage), the *plena cognitio divinorum*.[10] But that, however, amounts to saying that the glorified Christ continues to speak in the Church through the Spirit; the word transmitted to it through the Spirit is no other than the word of the Lord himself, and as a consequence in the gospel of John the word of the earthly and of the exalted Christ can no longer be distinguished at all; for the Spirit of course operates particularly in the inspired work of the evangelist, who presents to the Church Jesus's words as the words of the

glorified Christ (see also on this Section VIII). Blank, therefore, rightly says,[11] "Here the real principle of the Johannine
form of gospel becomes visible; in it a sharp distinction
between the historical Christ and the Christ who is disclosing
himself through the Spirit is no longer possible. The historical
Christ is the spiritual Christ and vice versa. Anyone who
affirms the contrary must also produce the criteria by which
the distinction can be made in John and that objectively, not
by subjective and arbitrary estimation".

Finally the unfolding of the full truth of Christ constitutes
that "glorification" of Jesus by the Spirit which Christ
announces at 16:14 ($\dot{\epsilon}\kappa\epsilon\hat{\iota}\nu\text{os}$ $\dot{\epsilon}\mu\dot{\epsilon}$ $\delta o\xi\acute{a}\sigma\epsilon\iota$). For this is not meant
to refer to the parousia[12] but, as is clear from the explanatory
clause which follows ("For he will take what is mine and
declare it to you"), it refers to the explicative function of the
Spirit. This means, however, that Jesus's *doxa* appears and
finds concrete expression in the apostolic Christology, which
by its very nature, of course, is at the same time doxology.
In it the Spirit already causes Jesus's authority "to shine forth
with power".[13] The fourth gospel itself bears witness how the
doxa of the Logos became "visible" (1:14) to the apostolic
eye-witnesses in the incarnate, and under the influence of the
inspiration of the Spirit of God, it causes Jesus's glory to shine
forth for the Church. The work of the evangelist is itself
doxology. In it Christ appears as the eternal Logos who has
been made flesh, and as such has returned to the glory of the
Father. The gospel mirrors the divine *doxa* of Jesus in its
Christological proclamation.

According to the fifth Paraclete saying, there also belongs
to the increase of his glory the communication of "what is

to come" (τὰ ἐρχόμενα ἀναγγελεῖ ὑμῖν). The term ἀναγγέλλειν, which appears three times in the fifth saying, properly means to give a report about something which one has experienced and heard, " to repeat what has been heard" (ἀν-αγγέλλειν), "to transmit a message",[14] and also simply "to announce", "proclaim" (and to that extent is equivalent in meaning to ἀπαγγέλλειν, cf. 1 Jn 1:3 with 1:5). As according to John 16:13–15, the Paraclete "receives" what belongs to Jesus, ἀναγγέλλειν in the fifth saying will rather have the meaning of transmitting a message received (cf. ὅσα ἀκούει, λαλήσει in the same verse). The message concerns "what is to come". What is meant by this? We inevitably think of the events of the Last Days. Wikenhauser would like to take the expression in the further sense "that the Paraclete also confers the gift of prophecy (1 Cor 13:8; 14:21–33; 1 Thess 5:19 f.; 1 Jn 4:1)". Probably, however, Thüsing is nearest the mark when he conjectures "that the announcing of the ἐρχόμενα is identical with the whole operation of the Spirit", and so sees in τὰ ἐρχόμενα a very wide term "which comprises the whole accomplishment of the work of salvation by the Spirit or, as the case may be, the disciples".[15] The Paraclete makes known the Church's future fundamentally in relation to Jesus Christ. He leads the Church into its future and ensures that the glory of Christ on high is ever present in it. The operation of the Paraclete signifies the other, new form of presence of the glorified Christ during his absence in earthly form.[16] According to the first saying (14:16 f.) this operation of the "Helper" never ceases in the Church; he remains "for ever" (εἰς τὸν αἰῶνα) with the Church. Through his function of declaring "all truth", the Spirit decisively contributes to building up the apostolic tradition in the Church. "In fact he is precisely the 'principle' of this apostolic tradition, the 'guarantee of its truth' through the 'bringing to mind' which he effects" (J. Blank).

This work of the Spirit undoubtedly had its particular outcome and enduring objective expression in the writing of the gospels, particularly John's gospel. Statements like the following: "The Johannine theology is an interpretation of the Gospel which has been prompted by the Spirit" (A. Loisy)[17] or even more the following: "Perhaps John's gospel is itself the message of the Paraclete . . ." and the message "is no other than the fourth gospel" (H. Sasse),[18] have much in their favour. A. Kragerud is even of the opinion that the beloved disciple "represents the Paraclete and in a certain way is his embodiment".[19] This opinion is, of course, undoubtedly an exaggeration; but it is certain that the author of the fourth gospel regarded his work as produced in collaboration and as springing from the "common" testimony of the Paraclete and the Church to Jesus Christ. The statement of the third Paraclete saying (15:26 f.), "He will bear witness to me and you also are witnesses", finds fulfilment in a special way in the work of the evangelist in the fourth gospel. "What the evangelist hears in the 'I am'-sayings, and sees represented in the signs, and unfolds in the discourses, whether in monologue or dialogue,[20] is interpretation of Jesus as this derives from the Paraclete" (W. Grundmann).[21] That also means, however, that the guiding principle, the *causa formalis*, of the Johannine act of seeing, as this was analysed in Section III, is the Paraclete. It is he who shapes the act of vision in such a way that it leads to true gnosis of the mystery of Christ. The Spirit guides the seeing, remembering, knowing, coming to know and bearing witness of the witnesses in such a way that they can make Jesus's *doxa* powerfully shine forth in their testimony in the Church and before the world. The Johannine mode of vision and the work of the Paraclete belong inseparably together.

VI

THE JOHANNINE MODE OF VISION AND THE TRADITION OF THE EARLY CHURCH

1. *Preliminary remarks*

The Johannine mode of vision led to a new interpretation of the history of Jesus. Did this come about on grounds of opposition to the Church's previous tradition about Jesus? E. Käsemann put forward a thesis of that kind.[1] According to him the Johannine writings must "be understood on the basis of the antithesis to incipient early Catholicism".[2] The author, according to Käsemann, is the "presbyter" of 3 John, who identified himself with the beloved disciple and in his gospel opposes the *Christus praesens* to a Jesus who is now envisaged only as the object of the Church's "tradition". Nevertheless, the presbyter was no enthusiast who rejected all tradition. But his relation to it was dialectical. "He did not allow tradition to replace the Spirit and make the *praesentia Christi* superfluous. Revelation for him is not an occurrence that is simply over and which the Church as an institute for salvation has to preserve. Past revelation may not be misused so as to reject and silence the *Christus praesens* as Judaism does. All tradition has meaning only as a summons to hear the voice of Christ in the present. It too remains essentially testimony, and consequently never exempts one from seeing, hearing and believing for oneself."[3] Whatever may be thought of Käsemann's arbitrary presbyter-hypothesis,[4] his attempt to support his thesis on the basis of the "doctrine of this man" merits attention.[5] Käsemann reduces it in essentials to the formula *Christus praesens*—"the real theme of the gospel"[6]— and there is no doubt that in this the Christ of the fourth gospel is correctly envisaged. But even though the beloved disciple, whom Käsemann regards as a projection of the presbyter,[7] may be a charismatically gifted figure (cf. Section V), he does not set his charisma in opposition to tradition. On the contrary, he represents precisely in matters of Christology the tradition taught "from the beginning" ($\dot{\alpha}\pi$' $\dot{\alpha}\rho\chi\hat{\eta}s$) as 1 John proves (cf. 1:1; 2:24: "Let what you heard from the beginning abide in you"; 3:11).[8] Scholars are coming to recognize more and more that while the fourth gospel certainly traces anew the history of Jesus, it is nevertheless not the completely independent project of a detached mind, but stands in various traditions, and they seek to throw light on these.[9] That also applies to his Christology, which for our present purpose does not require detailed treatment. Its chief aspects are pre-Johannine and common to the whole early Church (for example: pre-existence, incarnation, divine sonship, "Son of man",[10] submission to death for the world, resurrection, glorification). The relation of the fourth evangelist to the preceding apostolic and ecclesiastical tradition about Jesus cannot be described as "dialectical" but rather as interpretative.[11] John expounds anew the tradition known to him for his own purposes and in the perspective in which he sees the whole Christ-event. In this interpretation his mode of vision plays a decisive part. The author, however, does not isolate himself from the society of the Church but consciously stands within it. In the Johannine writings this feeling for the community finds expression particularly in the "We"-formula which occurs both in the gospel (cf. above all 1 : 14: "We have beheld his glory") and in the First Letter (cf. particularly 1 : 1-3; 4 : 14, 16). How does John understand the "We"-formula? Answering this question manifests a common domain of belief, in which the author of the fourth gospel stands, and leads on from there to the problem of the "hermeneutical circle". As regards the common domain of belief, the role of tradition in hermeneutical activity necessarily appears. Finally, reflection on these questions calls for comparison with the situation of the synoptics.

2. "We"-formula and act of vision

The "We"-formula in the Johannine writings was dealt with thoroughly by A. von Harnack.[12] As he correctly noted, it has various meanings. Our question here is how John understood the "We"-formula in the context of his act of vision. This will first be discussed on the basis of the classical text 1 : 14: καὶ ἐθεασάμεθα τὴν δόξαν αὐτοῦ. Does the "seeing" spoken of here only mean " the experience of Christian faith ", as W. G. Kümmel thinks (he refers to the plural ἐλάβομεν at verse 16)?[13] If that were so, one would surely rather expect it to be expressed in the present tense; for faith also continues to "see" in Jesus Christ the glory of the only-begotten of the Father.[14] Those who maintain that the author of the fourth gospel is the apostle John, the son of Zebedee, have no doubt that the verb ἐθεασάμεθα with its past tense is intended primarily to refer to the apostolic eye-witnesses of Jesus's life.[15] But what was said in Section III, 1, about seeing applies here. It is a believing sight which brings knowledge and which consequently could be transcribed into kerygma (cf. 1 John 1:3: "What we have seen and heard we proclaim also to you"). The "We"-circle, of which John knows himself a member, is, therefore, in the first place the society of the apostolic eye-witnesses and hearers. The kerygma as the enduring "product" of what the eye-witnesses and hearers "beheld" in Jesus the incarnate Logos, is the work of a fellowship which lives on in the Church as apostolic tradition. And so the seeing does not remain "limited to contemporaries, but is transmitted by this [tradition] to all subsequent generations; but it is transmitted only through that [tradition], for what is in question is not the contemplation of something timeless and eternally valid, but of the ὁ λόγος σὰρξ ἐγένετο" (Bultmann on John 1:14); we should prefer to say, of the *doxa* of the incarnate Logos. Bultmann is right in holding that the ἐθεασάμεθα does not designate "an assignable number of eye-witnesses" because, of course, through their intermediacy those who believe in the apostolic kerygma can also pronounce this ἐθεασάμεθα in faith, just as "the evangelist is aiming at transmitting such θεᾶσθαι by means of his gospel". But the "beholding" of those who believe the kerygma is to be distinguished from that of the eye-witnesses; it is to a certain extent a "secondary" view, causing the believers to share in seeing, by means of the kerygma, in the announcement of the eye-witnesses.[16] This is the reason why, as Bultmann aptly puts it, it is not possible

to speak of this "beholding" by the faithful apart from the
history established by the believing eye-witnesses. He also
observes, "The community which states it [the θεᾶσθαι]
is not constituted by an idea and eternal norms, but by a
concrete history and its tradition. The seeing cannot be
detached from this tradition." With this reference to tradition,
Bultmann provides a very important cue. The seeing of the
eye-witnesses leads via their kerygma, their declaration, to
tradition, to the διδαχή about Jesus Christ valid "from the
beginning" (cf. 1 John). Anyone who then places himself with
faith in the "We"-circle, affirms the Christological tradition
of the Church. Acceptance of the apostolic kerygma actually
establishes, according to 1 John 1 : 3, the κοινωνία of the faithful with the apostolic eye-witnesses and hearers: "What we
have seen and heard we proclaim also to you so that you may
have fellowship with us". Thus the author of the fourth gospel
consciously stands in the common domain of the Church's
faith; he expresses this by the "We"-formula.[17] What is the
significance of this for his mode of vision, for his comprehension of his subject, Jesus Christ?

3. The tradition of faith and the "hermeneutical circle"

By the fact that John did not write his gospel in opposition
to the "orthodox" tradition concerning Jesus, but expressly
intended to stand within the domain of the Church's belief
and existing tradition, he brought with him to his interpretation of the history of Christ a presupposition, namely the
assumption of the previous πίστις of the Church. This πίστις
involves for him a prior understanding, or as it might perhaps

more clearly be put, a precomprehension, not only in regard to the general primordial sense of man's situation in the world (see below on this), but specifically with respect to Christology. The Christ whom John interprets "already comes to him in a definite interpretation from the preceding πίστις of the Church. Consequently his interpretation of the figure of Christ is only the logical continuation of a process of interpretation which goes back much further. But if the domain of the Church's faith in which John deliberately places himself determined for him a Christological preconception which exerted decisive influence on his mode of vision, this is an instance of the law of the "hermeneutical circle".

Modern hermeneutics has occupied itself intensively with the problem of the "circle". The decisive impetus was given by M. Heidegger in *Sein und Zeit,* especially in §§ 32 (Comprehension and Explication) and 63 (The hermeneutical situation reached for an interpretation of the meaning of concern in relation to Being, and the methodological character of the existential analysis in general.).[18] According to Heidegger, there is constituted, simultaneously with the human being's feeling of his primordial situation in the world, a fundamental existential, i.e., structural characteristic of man's being as such,[19] which he calls comprehension. The human being, as comprehension, projects his being towards possibilities. "The projecting of comprehension involves the intrinsic possibility of its own unfolding. This unfolding of comprehension we call explication. In it comprehension by comprehending appropriates what it has comprehended."[20] Comprehension, therefore, precedes explicit interpretation, and is the condition of its possibility. "All explicit interpretation which seeks to bring about understanding must already have grasped in advance what is to be interpreted."[21] Consequently interpretation is "never a grasp of a datum without any presuppositions". Interpretation of "something precisely *as* something . . . is essentially grounded on prepossession, preview, preconception."[22] The conceptual apparatus which is employed in any interpretation has its ground in each case in preconception. Thus John's interpretation of the Christ-event is based on prepossession, preview and preconception, and the comprehension moves within these and the interpretation is guided by them. And for John, prepossession, preview and preconception in regard to the Christ-event were given by his origin in the "We"-circle of the apostolic eye-witnesses and hearers and in the Church and its tradition of belief. These themselves conveyed to him a definite conception of the Christ-event, which then continued to be operative in his interpretative exposition. Thus the Johannine interpretation of the Christ-event, from the hermeneutical point of view, moves in a circle. "But to regard this circle as a vicious circle and to look out for ways of avoiding it . . . is radically to misunderstand comprehension . . . . What is decisive is not to get out of the circle but to enter it in the proper way . . . . It conceals a positive possibility of attaining authentic knowledge" (Heidegger).[23]

The προάγων[24] seeks to break out of the circle. Of course he too brings his own precomprehension and preconception when he interprets the figure of Christ, but he regards the "circle" of the apostolic tradition of the Church as a vicious one; in his work of interpretation other "traditions" are operative, perhaps of a philosophical or mythological kind. And so his

Christ is projected as a completely new figure essentially different from that of tradition and in fact opposed to it.[25] This is just what does not happen with John; he derives the "prejudgment" which is operative in his interpretation of the figure of Christ, from the preceding Christological tradition of the Church. Of course the background of Johannine theology in the history of religions is of a very mixed kind, but the fundamental equation contained in the ancient profession of faith, "Jesus [crucified] = the Christ and Son of God", is consistently maintained as deliberate theme (Jn 20:31; 1 John). That is to say, the prejudgment is drawn from that apostolic tradition concerning Christ which is attested throughout the New Testament. John stands not outside but inside that tradition.[26] In fact, as J. M. Braun's work "Les grandes traditions et Israël, l'accord des écritures d'après le quatrième Évangile"[27] shows so clearly, John with his view of Christ stands in the stream of traditions which go back to the Old Testament.[28] And in regard to John, Gadamer's observation holds good: "Comprehension only achieves its true potentiality if the preconceptions which it brings into action are not arbitrary ones".[29] John does indeed draw his prepossession, preview and preconception from the reality itself, i.e., Jesus Christ, but that reality itself is a prior datum for him in the tradition of the Church; he stands in the "We"-circle of the Church; his prejudgment is not an arbitrary one. Thus he does not, hermeneutically speaking, leave the circle, but penetrates deeper into it. In this circular process there occurs, according to Gadamer, a profound movement, namely "the interplay of the movement of tradition and that of the interpreter".[30]

What is the function of tradition in this? The question is raised, of course, simply in regard to the fourth gospel.

4. *The function of tradition in hermeneutical activity*[31]

Since tradition transmits a prior comprehension, it conveys knowledge to those within its current. For anyone who preserves ($\tau\eta\rho\epsilon\hat{\imath}\nu$) a tradition—an important concept in Johannine thought[32]—and allows it to determine the horizon of his interpretation, tradition is not something alien. Reference to it makes knowing almost a recognition in which the past is wholly appropriated. In this way tradition becomes hermeneutically productive in the process of interpretation and the interpreter's creative power is not impeded.[33] The fourth gospel provides a typical example and confirmation of this. It handles portions of the preceding tradition of the Church regarding Jesus with dominating freedom, yet does not succumb to subjectivism; on the contrary, in the process of exposition it penetrates deeper and deeper into the active course of tradition. Gadamer notes,[34] "Understanding itself is to be regarded not so much as a subjective action as an insertion into a process of tradition in which past and present continually exercise mutual interaction".

Tradition implies, and at the same time anticipates, a certain *meaning* which becomes explicitly understood through the interpretation of tradition. The task here consists "of widening in concentric circles the unity of the meaning understood. Agreement of all details with the whole in each case is the criterion of understanding. Absence of such agreement signifies failure to understand" (Gadamer).[35] Thus in the fourth gospel the "meaning" which was implicit in the apostolic tradition of the Church regarding Jesus becomes explicitly understood. The antecedent "meaning" of the Christ-event and its tradition provides the guiding-line for understanding and interpretation;[36] what is "new" in John's contribution is integrated into and subordinated to it. All parts are brought into harmony with the whole, and, particularly in the fourth gospel, the whole permeates all the parts, even the language and style. "In each case it is only in such a whole of an objective and subjective kind that understanding can be perfectly achieved", Gadamer observes, and refers to W. Dilthey, who speaks of relation to a central point from which understanding of the whole follows.[37] The centre round which the fourth gospel in its entirety is composed, whether in its Christology, soteriology or eschatology, is the glorified Christ in whom, however, the historical Jesus Christ is not forgotten.[38]

Since understanding "primarily means apperceptive grasp of the subject-matter itself", the first of all hermeneutical requirements is "the precomprehension that springs from having to deal with the same thing" (Gadamer).[39] John is dealing with the "same thing" as the apostolic tradition of the Church: Jesus Christ; he is linked to it "by the community of decisive fundamental assumptions". Consequently hermeneutics must, according to Gadamer, "start from the fact that anyone who seeks to understand is linked to the matter which finds expression by being handed down, and that he either is or becomes connected with the tradition in which that expression occurs".[40] This applies in a high degree to the Johannine "comprehension" of the Christ-event; it is connected with the precomprehension of the apostolic tradition in which Jesus Christ "delivered" himself to the Church. Nevertheless, as the fourth gospel shows, this conscious attachment to a tradition does not mean its mechanical acceptance or its mere repetition, but a creative, very independent interpretation of it, to meet the needs of the situation in the history of theology and the Church at the time it was written (see Section II, 1). But the precomprehension, taken over from tradition and acknowledged, preserved the author of the fourth gospel from putting forward in his work a false interpretation of the history of Christ. This was acknowledged and confirmed by the Church itself, which at a very early date incorporated the Gospel according to John into the canon of scripture, whereas that was not done for instance in the case of the Gospel of Peter. This was done not simply because the author of the fourth gospel was, according to early conviction, the apostle John, but much more because the Church's sense of the faith perceived in it a legitimate interpretation of the history of Christ, and one that was linked to the preceding apostolic tradition.[41]

Here again the hermeneutical significance of the time-interval must once more be recalled.[42] Gadamer says of this, "The time-interval . . . alone brings out fully the true meaning that something involves".[43] "True meaning" in the case of the Johannine interpretation of the history of Christ is not a different meaning of the latter, but a deeper grasp, achieved above all by giving much stronger expression to its transcendent background, Christ's origin and goal. There is no contradiction to tradition involved in the fact that this "giving expression" has recourse to patterns of representation and statement and a conceptual apparatus which were not given absolutely as prior data in the Church's previous tradition regarding Jesus but originated elsewhere (in the world of dualism, for example). What Gadamer says of the interpretation of an historical text also applies *mutatis mutandis* to John's work of exegesis: "To want to avoid one's own terms in interpretation is not only impossible but a plain contradiction".[44] For "of course the very meaning of interpretation is 'to bring one's own previous ideas into play, so that the import of the text really finds expression for us' ".[45] Properly understood, another statement of Gadamer also applies to John:[46] " In every interpretation additional light is thrown". In the case of the fourth gospel this means that the "mystery of Christ" is *more clearly* expressed for the Church. This additionally *illuminating* interpretation is achieved with the help of a mode of vision directed by love and penetrating deep into the mystery under the guidance of the Paraclete.

The objection might be raised that form-history has brought to light that the synoptic tradition itself constitutes an interpretative account; how then does the synoptic interpretation of the history of Christ differ from the Johannine?

5. *Comparison with the synoptics*

The form-history of the synoptic gospels has made it clear that the tradition about Jesus which they have preserved is not the outcome of a mode of historical writing intended to be strictly biographical. In the synoptic tradition itself the post-paschal standpoint already exerts its influence, affecting even the transmission of Jesus's sayings. For even these already undergo a certain interpretation, even in the "gospel before the gospels". There was never a tradition purely for its own sake; it was always intended from the start as proclamation and testimony. G. Eichholz is entirely correct in saying that "the Jesus of scientific history would be an abstraction", and observes: "To bear witness faithfully does not mean to repeat tradition but to announce the gospel with the responsibility which the present time demands".[47] Similarly A. Vögtle says: "The postpaschal history of Jesus was . . . from the beginning a living tradition, which was affected by the deeper insight into the revelation of Christ gained from Good Friday and Easter, but also by the questions and vital needs of the early Church. That is to say, the transmission of the contents of the history of Jesus even in the pre-literary stage was a tradition orientated towards the present. To a certain extent, which varied of course from case to case, actualizing factors were involved in the reporting. Consequently elucidatory, interpretative touches and indications for practical application were admitted, corresponding to particular vital needs and questions of the early Church, its liturgical, missionary, catechetical, apologetical, disciplinary and other purposes."[48] The synoptic tradition is, therefore, to a certain extent an *interpretation* of the life and teaching of the Jesus of history. That also means, however, that the Johannine view of the history of Jesus, representing as it does to a considerable extent a new interpretation, is entirely in line with the process of comprehension and interpretation which set in at once after Easter. Consequently the difference that exists between the synoptic and Johannine presentation of the story of Christ cannot be reduced to the formula: the synoptics give it "as it historically occurred" whereas John interprets it in his own special way. We must rather say that both the synoptics and John present an *interpreted* life of Jesus. Nevertheless, of course, considerable difficulties remain. These seem to consist essentially of the following, apart altogether of course, from the question of contents: a) The time-interval, which is by no means unimportant for the interpretation of an historical event, is considerably greater for John than for the synoptics. b) The particular functional context in the Church's life is different for the composition of the fourth gospel from that of the synoptic gospels; its position in the history of theology and the Church is quite different (cf. Section II, 1). c) John writes his history of Christ in his own terminology, which is different from that of the synoptics. This terminology is not only found in the narrative portions of the fourth gospel but also in the discourses of the Johannine Christ. The Johannine Christ speaks John's language, and to such an extent that the question of the *ipsissima vox Jesu*, which in regard to the synoptic tradition is an entirely meaningful one, becomes almost without object, if not meaningless, in regard to the fourth gospel.

In brief, this means that the process of interpretation is carried very much further in John's gospel than in the synoptics. The Johannine mode of vision contributes decisively to determining this advance. In that way, however, the question of the Jesus of history clearly becomes more acute.

VII

THE JOHANNINE MODE OF VISION AND THE QUESTION OF THE JESUS OF HISTORY

1. *Preliminary remarks*

The Johannine Christ speaks John's language. This fact was the starting-point of all our reflections. It raises the question of the relation between the words of the Johannine Christ and those of the Jesus of history.

In answer it is possible to point out that the words of the Johannine Christ are words that have been interpreted with the assistance of the Paraclete. This has been repeatedly shown in the course of our discussion. It is a correct answer but is far from explaining everything. One might also point to the phenomenon of "Christ's language", which H. Schürmann has observed in our Lord's words in the synoptics,[1] and which can be observed to an even greater degree in our Lord's words in John's gospel, for instance in the "I"-sayings of the Johannine Christ.[2] One could also point to the "dualist" terminology of John's gospel,[3] and explain this from the history of religions (by reference, for example, to the language of early gnosticism which John causes his Christ to speak).[4] All three answers have a certain justification but are not sufficient to explain in a fully satisfactory way the fact that the

Johannine Christ speaks Johannine language. The feeling is inescapable that more far-reaching explanations are called for.

Are the Johannine language and mode of speech connected with the Johannine mode of vision and if so how? An *attempt* will be made, in what follows, to find an answer to this question. But in order to arrive at a full answer, account must be taken of the special unity that exists in John's gospel between the Jesus of history and the glorified Christ.

2. *Johannine mode of vision and Johannine language*

The Johannine mode of vision, in the comprehensive sense which has been worked out in this *quaestio disputata,* extends, it would seem, to the eternal dimensions of the historical figure of Jesus, those which reach into the divine mystery of the Logos. In this way it makes possible the transposition of what has been "seen", "known" and "heard", into the testimony of the gospel kerygma which renders it present. The Johannine act of vision makes possible a process of kerygmatic transposition. That was the conclusion of our inquiry in Section III. Now this process comprises both Jesus's words (the Johannine discourses of Christ) and his work (especially his σημεῖα). For the Johannine accounts of σημεῖα also serve the Christ kerygma and manifest Jesus's *doxa* (cf. for example Jn 2:11; 11:40),[5] just as his words are the ῥήματα τοῦ θεοῦ (3:34; 14:10; 17:8).

The last and decisive reason that makes the Johannine act of vision possible seems to be that for John the incarnation of the Logos and his whole historical words and deeds possess an epiphany character; in them the *doxa* of the eternal Logos is revealed. The act of vision grasps the "manifestation" in the incarnate Logos (1:14) of what is recognized by faith and gives kerygmatic expression to this in the testimony of "remembrance". If this transposition into kerygmatic language was adequately to be carried out, it could only be done in an appropriate terminology. Now the Johannine language—inevitably, we must say—is rich in terms capable of giving expression to the epiphany occurrence. Johannine language is to a great extent the language of epiphany. Only brief reference can be made to this point here; it would merit a detailed study in itself.[6] We might note the role played by explicit epiphany words, for example δόξα, φῶς, φαίνειν φανεροῦν, φανεροῦσθαι, (ἐξ-)έρχεσθαι, χαταβαίνειν, ἀποστέλλειν, πέμπειν, which are all connected with the appearance in the world of the Logos-Christ, and to which there corresponds on man's part "seeing" and "hearing" in faith. Now in Old Testament descriptions of theophanies, "seeing" and "hearing" belong to the theophany occurrence. "He who has seen me has seen the Father" (14:9): Christ is the appearance of the Father in the world. He is the Son and envoy of the Father (*passim*). He is the Son of man who has descended from heaven (3:13). He is the incarnate Logos (1:14). Precisely because in the fourth gospel the Christ-event is very markedly understood as a "vertical" event taking place between heaven and earth, it has throughout the character of an epiphany.[7] Such an event is above all "seen", and what is "seen" (and "heard") in it by faith is more than the immediate historical surface, it is the heavenly *doxa* of the divine Logos himself. Precisely what has been "beheld" and "heard" and so "known" in the testimony of "remembrance" is transposed into the kerygma and in this transposition what has "shown" itself in the epiphany of the Christ-event finds expression. It does so in the terminology most appropriate to the occurrence, that of epiphany itself. The Christ-event understood as an epiphany, with John, in the process of kerygmatical trans- position becomes the gospel "testimony" formulated in terms of epiphany. In this way the "knowledge" of Christ attained in the original act of vision of the apostolic eye-witnesses is completely carried over into the process of kerygmatic utterance.[8] The proper achievement of language, according to Gadamer, is the "merging of horizons which occurs in under- standing",[9] without the reference to attested history having to be abandoned thereby. In the fourth gospel this reference is actually established in a very living and conscious way, as more than thirty concrete topographical indications[10] prove. In this way, in the "remembrance" which is what the gospel essentially is, the eternal, permanently valid element of the Christ-event is preserved for the Church. Because however this eternal, permanently valid element showed itself precisely in the incarnate Logos who appeared in the world, that is to say, in the historical Jesus, what is attested remains always linked to *history* and so the unity of the kerygmatic Christ with the historical Jesus is maintained and also the time-interval. Precisely in the Johannine stamp of the terminology of Christ's discourses in the fourth gospel, Jesus speaks in such a way that what was manifested in his words and works to the apostolic act of vision, is preserved for the Church. So in John's gospel there speaks the incarnate Logos and Son of God, who appeared in the world but did not remain in the world, who returned in glory to the Father, and who as glorified continues to speak through the Paraclete in the Church and in the gospel.

3. The essential identity of the Jesus of history with the glorified Christ

This point can be dealt with briefly because valuable results of research are already available, especially the thorough investigation of W. Thüsing, *Die Erhöhung und Verherrlichung Jesu im Johannesevangelium*.[11] "The use of the term δοξάζειν, both for Jesus's work on earth and for the saving process which is accomplished after his departure to his Father, indicates that between these two stages there is a relation of analogy and that in the Johannine view the saving work of both stages forms a unity" (Thüsing).[12] The revelation of Jesus through the Paraclete is, according to John 14:26, "a deepening repetition or, rather, the actual accomplishment on the new level of universal efficacy ".[13] "The revelation-event of Jesus's earthly life and that of the Paraclete are not two different works, but the one work of Jesus himself in its two phases of realization."[14] This means that the operation of the Jesus of history and that of the glorified Christ form a unity, a complete whole, and its two "stages" are "in a number of ways projected into one another " by the evangelist (Thüsing).[15] Fundamentally, therefore, it is impossible to say that in John's gospel the "historical" Jesus acts and speaks until the crucifixion, and after Easter the "glorified" Christ acts and speaks; the glorified Christ already acts and speaks all the time in the words and work of the "historical" (prepaschal)

Jesus. The classical examples of this are perhaps Christ's discourses in chapters 3, 6 and 17. Both the prepaschal and the postpaschal Christ speak the same language, and it is Johannine. The ground of the identity of both lies in Johannine Christology. According to Johannine teaching, Jesus is the Logos who has come from God's eternity and who, after his death on the Cross, returns to the eternal glory of the Father. John sees no absolute break either in the incarnation of the Logos or in Jesus's death; for the incarnation is the coming and appearance of the Logos in the world and Jesus's death is his transit to the Father. There is a continuous line from pre-existence, through incarnation and death to glorification. This is the ontological ground which ultimately permits the evangelist to cause the glorified Christ to speak in the pre-paschal Jesus. Consequently we are justified in saying that in John's gospel Christ proclaims himself.[16]

More precisely, Christ after his glorification continues to speak into the Church through the instrument of his revelation, the Paraclete, and the latter through the evangelist. The evangelist, therefore, is the inspired mouthpiece of the one Christ through whom the latter speaks in Johannine language and gives answers to the questions which had arisen in the Church at the time the gospel was composed.[17] The answer, however, is at the same time a rendering explicit of what had been taught from the beginning in the Church about Christ. Through the *Christus praesens* of the fourth gospel, the apostolic tradition about Jesus going back to the beginning is not annulled, but rather made truly actual and interpreted anew. Jesus's earthly life is represented as the epiphany of the *doxa* of the divine Logos "beheld" by the believing eye-witnesses and hearers and "as the Father's word of love to the faithful spoken and lived by Jesus" (E. Haenchen).[18] But it was only understood in this way by the believers in the light of Jesus's resurrection from the dead and because of the sending of the Spirit, the special gift of the glorified Christ to the Church (Jn 7:39; 20:22). "By reason of this new gift the evangelist transcribed the proclamation of the earthly Jesus in conformity with the new Christ-reality" (Haenchen),[19] and he did this *sub inspiratione Spiritus Sancti.*

VIII

JOHANNINE MODE OF VISION AND INSPIRATION

In this last chapter of our *quaestio*, we are concerned above all with the problem how the nature of inspiration is to be understood in relation to John's gospel, in view of the findings of our inquiry. A special difficulty resulting from the form-history view of the gospels seems frequently to arise from the dogma of inspiration. How is the fact that John makes his Christ speak Johannine language compatible with inspiration? After all, by his introductory formulas, expressed in the past tense (for example, "Jesus answered"), John seems to intend to declare that the words of Jesus which follow are the words of the historical Jesus. The present writer knows by experience that this objection is frequently put forward in discussions after lectures on the Jesus of history in the gospels. It is, therefore, necessary to deal with the matter briefly by way of conclusion.

A solution is not excessively difficult provided that what the Church's teaching on inspiration really says is correctly grasped.[1] It contains two principles: a) "The sacred writer is . . . not a merely mechanical instrument writing from 'dictation', but God acts upon him in such a way that with full knowledge, free will and the full use of his individual endowments and powers, he writes what God wills and how God wills it." b) "From the collaboration between God and the sacred writer it follows in the first place that the book produced in this way will reflect the knowledge, character and individuality of its human author and will also depend on him for its line of thought, literary composition and linguistic presentation" (Bea).[2] In applying these principles to John's gospel, one must in the first place start from the established facts. Now these clearly show that the Johannine Christ speaks John's language. It is to be inferred that this is in accord with the will of the inspiring Spirit of God (principle a); further, that John's gospel is dependent on its author for its linguistic presentation, even in the discourses of Christ (principle b). Since, according to John's gospel, it is the Paraclete through whom the glorified Christ "brings to remembrance" for the Church all that Jesus has said (cf. Section V), the Johannine words of Christ are those that the Spirit of truth in the Church by this activity of bringing to remembrance presents and interprets. But he presents and interprets them in such a way that the Johannine mode of vision is brought fully into operation, even in the linguistic respect, and as a consequence the Johannine Christ in fact speaks John's language. As moreover for John the Jesus of history and the glorified Christ are essentially identical (cf. VII, 2), it is also this one, indivisible Christ who speaks in the Johannine revelation-discourses.

John, however, also stands in the "We"-circle of the community of the apostolic Church; he consciously affirms its tradition (cf. Section VI). The Christ who in that tradition had already undergone a certain interpretation lives on in the "new" interpretation of the fourth gospel. The significance of belonging in this way to the heart of the tradition of the early Church for the question of the inspiration of a New Testament sacred author has been investigated in particular by K. Rahner. Even though there is no collective inspiration, it cannot, according to Rahner, be denied "that a written work clearly mirrors the character of the milieu in which its human author writes". Nor is it decided "whether the work was not in fact caused from the first by God *as* a regulative expression of that community's awareness of its faith".[3] The milieu in which John's gospel came into existence was essentially determined by two or perhaps three factors. The first of these was the preceding tradition of the apostolic and early Church, particularly as regards Christology, in which John also lived (cf. Section VI). Furthermore, as some at the present time conjecture, there was a tradition cultivated in "Johannine" churches and in it a certain terminology was developed which survives in the language of the fourth gospel.[4] Finally, there were the questions raised at the period when the gospel was composed, and which the gospel is intended to answer (cf. Section II, 1). At all events the author of the fourth gospel lived in a definite milieu, which influenced his system of ideas and images and his language and style. Since the Church received his work into the canon of New Testament writings, it thereby recognized and acknowledged that in it too the early Church's consciousness of its faith had received a regulative expression, behind which there stands the inspiration of the Spirit of God. God willed the early Church and also John's gospel, and willed it as it was put forward by its author for the Church: as the "maturest testimony to Christ of the primitive Church" (Schnackenburg),[5] as the "final [apostolic] knowledge of Jesus" (Kahlefeld).[6]

IX

SUMMARY

1. The Johannine Christ speaks John's language.
2. John's gospel answers questions raised at the time of its composition, particularly in regard to Christology.
3. Time-interval and "horizon" or perspective are of hermeneutical importance for the Johannine interpretation of the history of Jesus.
4. The Johannine act of vision, the "historical reason" of the fourth evangelist, can be successfully analysed by means of the gnoseological terminology he employs.
5. This analysis shows the possibility of transporting the knowledge attained in this act of vision into the kerygma attested and living on in the Church as "remembrance".
6. The Paraclete is the guiding principle in the Johannine act of vision, in which, moreover, ἀγάπη also shows its efficacy.
7. The Johannine mode of vision is also supported *materialiter* and *formaliter* by the tradition of the early Church, which provided a prejudgment which the evangelist adopted from the society of the "We"-circle to which he himself belonged.
8. The Johannine mode of vision deepened the early Church's knowledge of Christ, by rendering present in

the gospel through the Paraclete the "remembrance" of the Christ-event and so maintaining the "situation" of Jesus in the Church and the world.

9. In John's gospel Christ continues to proclaim himself; for this purpose the evangelist "lends" him his language which itself is an adequate expression of the epiphany-character of the Christ-event.

10. The very fact that the Johannine Christ speaks John's language is in accord with the Church's teaching about the inspiration of scripture.

ABBREVIATIONS

BZ   *Biblische Zeitschrift.*

LTK   *Lexikon für Theologie und Kirche* (2nd edition: 1957-65).

TLZ   *Theologische Literaturzeitung.*

TWNT   G. Kittel, ed., *Theologisches Wörterbuch zum Neuen Testament* (1933 ff.).
E.T.: *Theological Dictionary of the New Testament,* vol. I (1964) and vol. II (1965).

TZ   *Theologische Zeitschrift.*

ZNW   *Zeitschrift für die neutestamentliche Wissenschaft und die Kunde der älteren Kirche.*

NOTES

SECTION I

[1] Cf. my demonstration of the Johannine character of the language of the Paraclete sayings in *BZ*, new series, 5 (1961), pp. 56-70.

[2] Cf. for example F. Mussner, "Der historische Jesus und der Christus des Glaubens", in *BZ*, new series, 1 (1957), pp. 224-52; J. R. Geiselmann, *Die Frage nach dem historischen Jesus* (1965).

[3] *Wahrheit und Methode. Grundzüge einer philosophischen Hermeneutik* (1960). On the problems concerning hermeneutics much discussed at the present time, see also the important article of G. Ebeling in *Die Religion in Geschichte und Gegenwart* ([3]1957 ff.), III, col. 242-62 (with comprehensive bibliography), and also: *Archiv für Begriffsgeschichte. Bausteine zu einem historischen Wörterbuch der Philosophie* I (1955), p. 199 (with bibliography); *Reallexikon der deutschen Literaturgeschichte* I, article "Interpretation" (with bibliography); *Herméneutique et Tradition. Actes du Colloque International Rome*, 10-16 January 1963 (1963); R. Marlé, *Le problème théologique de l'herméneutique* (1963); R. Schnackenburg, "Zur Auslegung der Heiligen Schrift in unserer Zeit" in *Bibel und Leben* 5 (1964), pp. 220-36.

SECTION II

[1] Cf. for example A. Wikenhauser, *Einleitung in das Neue Testament* ([4]1961), p. 227; E.T.: *New Testament Introduction* (1963).

[2] Cf. *BZ*, new series, 1 (1957), pp. 236 f.

[3] On this cf. J. Sint, "Die Eschatologie des Täufers, die Täufergruppen und die Polemik der Evangelien" in *Vom Messias zum Christus* (1964), pp. 55-163 (126 ff.).

⁴ Cf. also R. Schnackenburg, *Die Johannesbriefe* (²1963), pp. 16–23; E. Schweizer, "Das johanneische Zeugnis vom Herrenmahl" in *Evangelische Theologie* 12 (1952/3), pp. 341–66.

⁵ Cf. the "apostolic" plural ἐθεασάμεθα at 1:14. Further details on this below, III, 1 and VI, 2.

⁶ Cf. Gadamer, *Wahrheit und Methode*, pp. 275–83.

⁷ *Ibid.*, p. 279.

⁸ Cf. *ibid.*, p. 281.

⁹ Cf. on this Gadamer, *op. cit.*, pp. 286–90.

¹⁰ *Ibid.*, p. 288.

¹¹ *Ibid.*, p. 289.

¹² *Ibid.*, p. 290.

SECTION III

¹ Some preliminary work on the term "seeing" has been done by O. Cullmann. See his essay, "Aux sources de la Tradition chrétienne", in *Mélanges Goguel* (1950), pp. 52–61.

² *Das Evangelium des Johannes* (⁶1959) on Jn 1:14.

³ Cf. on this Section VI, 2 below.

⁴ *Die Idee des Martyriums in der alten Kirche* (1936), p. 37, note 2.

⁵ "Glauben, Erkennen, Lieben nach dem Johannesevangelium" in *Besinnung auf das Neue Testament* (1964), pp. 279–93 (283).

⁶ Cf. also E. Käsemann, "Aufbau und Anliegen des johanneischen Prologs" in *Festschrift für F. Delekat* (1957), pp. 75–99 (93–95).

⁷ *Ibid.*, pp. 100 f.

⁸ Cf. R. Schnackenburg, *Die Johannesbriefe* on this passage.

⁹ The ontological possibility of this lies in the act of sight itself, for "seeing" itself always implies an interpretation; M. Heidegger expresses this state of affairs as follows: "All sight pure and simple, prior to any prediction . . . is in itself already comprehensive-interpretative" (*Sein und Zeit*, p. 149).

¹⁰ On the relation between sight and faith in the story of Thomas (Jn 20: 24–29), cf. H. Wenz, "Sehen und Glauben bei Johannes" in *TZ* 17 (1961), pp. 17–25. Wenz shows that in the story of Thomas seeing and faith are not two "radical opposites", as Bultmann maintains in his commentary on John (539, note 3).

[11] Cf. also G. Kittel in: *TWNT* I, pp. 216–22 (bibliography); J. Gnilka, "Zur Theologie des Hörens nach den Aussagen des Neuen Testamentes" at the Conference on Homiletics, Würzburg, 1960; H. Schlier, *loc. cit.*, pp. 280 f. It is remarkable that the key word "hearing" (biblical uses) is lacking in the *Lexikon für Theologie und Kirche* and the *Bibeltheologisches Wörterbuch* of J. B. Bauer as well as in the index of G. von Rad's *Old Testament Theology*. For the Old Testament, however, cf. now A. K. Fenz, *Auf Jahwes Stimme hören. Eine biblische Begriffsuntersuchung*, Wiener Beiträge zur Theologie, 6 (1964); cf. also note 13 below.

[12] *Sein und Zeit*, p. 163.

[13] The expression "to hear the voice" has its model in the Old Testament in the expression "to hear the voice of Yahweh", which is found particularly frequently in Deuteronomy; on this see J. Blank, *Krisis. Untersuchungen zur johanneischen Christologie und Eschatologie* (1964), p. 141, note 76.

[14] "Glauben, Erkennen, Lieben" (cf. note 5 above), pp. 281 ff.

[15] Cf. for example F. Mussner, *ZΩH* (1952), pp. 171–6; R. Schnackenburg in *LTK*, III, cols. 996–1000 (bibliography).

[16] *Das Evangelium nach Johannes* ([2]1957), p. 247.

[17] *Das Evangelium des Johannes*, p. 290.

[18] Cf. R. Schnackenburg, "Die 'situationsgelösten' Redestücke in Joh. 3" in *ZNW*, 49 (1958), pp. 88–99.

[19] Bultmann formulates this state of affairs as follows (*TWNT*, I, p. 712): "Clearly the author is opposing people who claimed a vision of God and a knowledge of God free from history"; and he points out the apparently dogmatic way "in which ὅτι clauses describe the content of the γινώσκειν : what is at issue is a *dogma* (a διδαχή Jn 7:16 f.), the dogma of Jesus's divine Sonship (7:26; 10:38; 14:20; 16:3; 17:7 f., 23, 25, etc.). It is in truth a matter of the historicity of revelation, but from it there follows the 'scandal' of dogmatic knowledge".

[20] Cf., for example, Barrett (*The Gospel according to St John*, [3]1958), Wikenhauser and Bultmann on this passage.

[21] Cf. also on this H. Schürmann, "Joh 6:51 c—ein Schlüssel zur grossen johanneischen Brotrede" in *BZ*, new series, 2 (1958), pp. 244–62; T. Müller, *Das Heilsgeschehen im Johannesevangelium* (no date given).

22 According to Wikenhauser, "the simplest and most obvious explanation is that the evangelist formulated what the Baptist said on the basis of the early Christian understanding of the work of redemption".

23 Cf. Bultmann, *loc. cit.,* p. 447 ("precisely in the coming of the Spirit he himself comes"); Wikenhauser on verse 20.

24 Cf. Bultmann on this passage.

25 *Herrlichkeit und Einheit. Eine Auslegung des Hohepriesterlichen Gebets (Johannes 17),* Die Welt der Bibel, 14 (1962), p. 68.

26 Cf. also Schnackenburg, *Die Johannesbriefe,* p. 154, note 1.

27 Cf. above, p. 3.

28 The reading πάντες is to be preferred to πάντα; further details on this in Schnackenburg, *Die Johannesbriefe,* p. 154.

29 Christological themes appear explicitly as the objects of οἴδαμεν at Jn 4:42 ("We know that this is indeed the Saviour of the world") and at 1 Jn 5:20 ("We know that the Son of God has come").

30 Cf. Schnackenburg on the passage.

31 Cf. on these terms H. Strathmann in *TWNT,* IV, pp. 477–520; N. Brox, *Zeuge und Martyrer. Untersuchungen zur frühchristlichen Zeugnis-Terminologie* (1961), pp. 70–92; J. Blank, *Krisis* (see note 13 above), pp. 198–226.

32 Cf. especially J. Blank.

33 *Krisis,* p. 215.

34 *SBΘW* sah Origen; χατέφαγεν is the reading of φ it Vg syrsin pesh boh Eusebius (and also most mss. of the Septuagint).

35 Cf. also 15:25; 19:28; Rom 11:9; 15:3; Acts 1:20.

36 Cf. also Wikenhauser on the passage.

37 Bultmann takes this view.

38 Cf. Ezek 40–44; Tob 13:11 ff.; 14:7 ff.; and also Ethiopic Henoch 90, 27 ff.

39 Further details on this in F. Mussner, " 'Kultische' Aspekte im johanneischen Christusbild" in *Liturgisches Jahrbuch* 14 (1964), pp. 185–200 (especially 190 f.).

40 τοῦ σώματος αὐτοῦ is in my view a genitive of content (definition).

41 "To the ἐγερθῆναι 2:22 corresponds the δοξασθῆναι 12:16" (Bultmann on the passage).

42 Bultmann also takes this view.

43 "What at John 2:22; 12:16; cf. 7:39, holds good of the 'remem-

brance' of a single saying of Jesus, namely that it was only understood by his disciples when Jesus had entered into his *doxa,* is to be understood as a general pattern and holds good of all the 'bringing to remembrance' by the Spirit" (H. Schlier, "Zum Begriff des Geistes nach dem Johannesevangelium" in *Besinnung auf das Neue Testament,* p. 267).
[44] Cf. on this Gadamer, *op. cit.,* pp. 324-60.

EXCURSUS

[1] Cf. on this in particular H. Zirker, "Die kultische Vergegenwärtigung der Vergangenheit in den Psalmen" in *Bonner Biblische Beiträge,* 20 (1964); and also W. Schottroff, *"Gedenken" im Alten Orient und im Alten Testament* (1964); Cl. Westermann, "Vergegenwärtigung in den Psalmen" in *Zwischenstation. Festschrift für K. Kupisch zum 60. Geburtstag* (1963), pp. 253-80; H. Gross, "Zur Wurzel *zkr*" in *BZ* 4 (1960), pp. 227-37; P. A. H. de Boer, *Gedenken und Gedächtnis in der Welt des Alten Testaments* (1962); N. A. Dahl, "Anamnesis. Mémoire et Commémoration dans le christianisme primitif" in *Studia Theologica,* 1 (1948), pp. 69-95.

[2] Cf. especially Zirker's observations in his section B III, 5 ("The commemorative liturgy in its power of uniting the ages", divided as follows: (a) "Seeing" the deeds of Yahweh as living encounter with the past that is proclaimed, (b) Remembrance of sin in the "We" which unites the generations, (c) Bridging the time-interval by representation by dramatic speech and (d) The relation between the uniqueness of the historical fact and its significance present in the liturgy.)

[3] *Ibid.,* p. 97.

[4] Cf. *ibid.*

[5] *Ibid.,* p. 98.

[6] *Ibid.,* p. 101.

[7] Cf. *ibid.,* pp. 101-5.

[8] *Ibid.,* p. 104.

[9] Cf. *ibid.,* pp. 105-9.

[10] *Ibid.,* p. 106.

[11] *Ibid.,* p. 107.

[12] *Ibid.*, p. 108.

[13] Cf. *ibid.*, pp. 109–18.

[14] Cf. *ibid.*, pp. 111 f.

[15] *Ibid.*, p. 112; cf. also W. Eichrodt, "Heilserfahrung und Zeitverständnis im Alten Testament" in *TZ*, 12 (1956), pp. 103–25 (116).

[16] *Ibid.*, p. 113.

[17] Cf. *ibid.*, p. 115.

[18] Cf. for example Deuteronomy 8:2 with 9:3.

[19] *Ibid.*, p. 117.

[20] *Ibid.*, p. 118.

[21] Cf. on this what we have to say on p. 71.

[22] So we read in the Constitution on the Sacred Liturgy of Vatican II, I, 7: "He (Christ) is present in his word, since it is he himself who speaks when the holy scriptures are read in the Church." Cf. also I, 33.

[23] On this cf. also section VI below.

[24] Cf. on this also O. Michel in *TWNT*, IV, pp. 686 f.; W. Marxsen, *Der Evangelist Markus* (²1959), pp. 83–92; G. Koch, "Dominus praedicans Christum—id est Jesus praedicatum" in *Zeitschrift für Theologie und Kirche*, 57 (1960), pp. 238–73; H. Schürmann, "Evangelienschrift und kirchliche Unterweisung. Die repräsentative Funktion der Schrift nach Lk 1, 1–4" in *Miscellanea Erfordiana* (1962), pp. 48–73.

[25] Schürmann, *loc. cit.*, p. 66.

[26] *Ibid.*, p. 69.

[27] Cf. *ibid.*, p. 72.

[28] *Besinnung auf das Neue Testament*, p. 267, note 11; cf. also Blank, *op. cit.*, pp. 141 and 268.

SECTION IV

[1] Particularly in his great essay "Liebe und Erkenntnis" in *Schriften zur Soziologie und Weltanschauungslehre*, I (1923), pp. 110–47. Important observations on the theme are also found in his work "*Wesen und Formen der Sympathie*" (²1923).

[2] *Die Johannesbriefe*, on the passage.

[3] Schnackenburg on the passage: "God's love has 'appeared', i.e.,

entered the domain of experience, by his sending his only Son into the world. The author consciously chooses this expression for God's self-revelation, because he is thinking of the 'appearance' in person of the Son of God (cf. 1:2; 3:5, 8), in whom God's love—and also God's life—as it were manifests itself. It is only through this, but perfectly through this, that God's hidden nature has become knowable."

[4] On him, see in particular in addition to the commentaries on the Gospel according to John, F. M. Braun, *Jean le Théologien et son évangile dans l'Église ancienne* (1959), pp. 301–30; A. Kragerud, *Der Lieblingsjünger im Johannesevangelium* (1959); H. Schlier, "Zum Begriff des Geistes nach dem Johannesevangelium" in *Besinnung auf das Neue Testament*, p. 264; W. Grundmann, *Zeugnis und Gestalt des Johannesevangeliums*, Arbeiten zur Theologie, no. 7, pp. 16–20.

[5] Cf. Jn 1:18.

[6] Cf. *Der Lieblingsjünger im Johannesevangelium*, p. 129 and also p. 114.

[7] *Ibid.*, p. 149. As regards criticism of this view, see R. Schnackenburg in *BZ*, new series, 4 (1960), pp. 302–7; W. Michaelis in *TLZ*, 85 (1960), 667–9.

[8] *Ibid.*, p. 18.

[9] "Zum Begriff des Geistes nach dem Johannesevangelium", *loc. cit.*, p. 269.

[10] Cf. *Der Lieblingsjünger im Johannesevangelium*, pp. 144 f.

[11] Cf. for further details my essay "Die johanneischen Parakletssprüche und die apostolische Tradition" in *BZ*, 5 (1961), p. 67, note 30.

[12] *Wesen und Formen der Sympathie*, p. 193.

[13] Cf. also R. Bultmann in *TWNT*, I, p. 711.

[14] "Seeing" as John understands it, if interpreted in terms of a philosophy of man's ontological constitution, is of course "encounter". Then what M. Heidegger has to say (*Sein und Zeit*, p. 147) is relevant: " 'Seeing' does not only mean perception with the bodily eyes, nor the simple awareness of something that is merely there. For the meaning of sight in terms of a philosophy of man's ontological constitution the only characteristic involved is that sight permits direct and open encounter with the particular being itself accessible to it." The beloved disciple "sees" Jesus in his mystery, because he meets Jesus directly as he is in himself; for this unreserved love is needed.

[15] Cf. my essay on "Die johanneischen Parakletssprüche und die apostolische Tradition", *passim*; J. L. Leuba, "Der Zusammenhang zwischen Geist und Tradition im Neuen Testament" in *Kerygma und Dogma*, 4 (1958), pp. 234-50.

SECTION V

[1] I follow here in essentials my essay "Die johanneischen Parakletssprüche und die apostolische Tradition", *loc. cit.*, pp. 56-70 (with bibliography); cf. also R. Schnackenburg's article "Paraklet" in *LTK*, VIII, cols. 77 f. (with bibliography); O. Betz, *Der Paraklet* (1963); M. Miguéns, *El Paráclito (Jn* 14-16), Stud. Bibl. Francisc., Anal. 2 (1963); *TWNT*, V. pp. 789-812 (J. Behm); Blank, *op. cit.*, pp. 316-32; Schlier, "Zum Begriff des Geistes nach dem Johannesevangelium", *loc. cit.*, pp. 264-78.

[2] Cf. Schnackenburg, *Die Johannesbriefe,* on the passage; K. H. Rengsdorf in *TWNT*, II, p. 146.

[3] *Das Evangelium des Johannes* on the passage.

[4] I expressed a different view in *BZ* (1961), p. 60.

[5] Cf. on this also Blank (*op. cit.*, pp. 317-25), who critically discusses the various explanations, based on comparative religion, of the Paraclete as presented by John; these have misrepresented John's thought in various ways. The connection of the Paraclete with Jesus is shown above all in the idea of mission: Jesus himself sends him or the Father sends him in his name (cf. 14:26; 15:26; 16:7).

[6] *Krisis*, p. 332.

[7] Cf. also Acts 5:32 ("We are witnesses to these things, and so is the Holy Spirit . . ."); Y. M. J. Congar, "Le St. Esprit et le corps apostolique réalisateurs de l'oeuvre du Christ" in *Revue des sciences philosophiques et théologiques,* 36 (1952), pp. 613-25; 37 (1953), pp. 24-48.

[8] It would also be worthy of note if the reading ἀκούσει (B D E H W $θ^1$ al; Or., Epiph., Eus., Cyr. Jer.) were the original; probably, however, this reading is a later assimilation to the "style of promise" of the other future tenses in the Paraclete sayings.

[9] *Die Erhöhung und Verherrlichung Jesu im Johannesevangelium*, Neutestamentliche Abhandlungen, no. 21 (1961), p. 147.

[10] Quoted in Blank, *op. cit.*, p. 331, note 46.

[11] *Ibid.*

[12] Barrett (on the passage) considers that it does.

[13] "To cause to shine forth powerfully" is how H. Schlier attempts to render the "untranslatable" term δοξάζειν ("Zum Begriff des Geistes nach dem Johannesevangelium", *loc. cit.*, p. 268). The term, like that of ὁδηγεῖν, has a certain prehistory, in connection with the notion of the Paraclete, in the Qumran writings; on this cf. O. Betz, *Der Paraklet*, pp. 91–94 and 100–6.

[14] Cf. P. Joüon in *Recherches de science religieuse*, 28 (1938), pp. 234 f.; see also ἀναγγελλειν in H. Liddell and R. Scott, *Greek-English Lexicon* (1925 ff.).

[15] *Erhöhung und Verherrlichung*, pp. 149–53.

[16] Cf. Blank, *op. cit.*, p. 333.

[17] Le quatrième Évangile (²1921), p. 432.

[18] *ZNW*, 24 (1925), pp. 273 f.

[19] *Der Lieblingsjünger*, p. 82.

[20] And what is "unfolded" in particular in Jesus's discourses in John is Christology. The form of speech and reply in the fourth gospel is a way of making Christology explicit.

[21] *Zeugnis und Gestalt*, p. 19.

SECTION VI

[1] "Ketzer und Zeuge. Zum johanneischen Verfasserproblem" in *Exegetische Versuche und Besinnungen*, I (1960), pp. 168–87.

[2] *Ibid.*, p. 182.

[3] *Ibid.*, p. 185.

[4] Cf. for criticism of this hypothesis, Schnackenburg, *Die Johannesbriefe*, pp. 299 f.; W. G. Kümmel, *Einleitung in das Neue Testament* (¹²1963), p. 327 ("untenable").

[5] "Ketzer und Zeuge", *loc. cit.*, p. 177.

[6] *Ibid.*, p. 181, note 42.

[7] Cf. *ibid.*, p. 180.

[8] How important for John the idea of tradition is in matters of the creed, has been shown by H. Conzelmann: "Was von Anfang war" in *Neutestamentliche Studien für R. Bultmann,* supplement (no. 21) of *ZNW* (1957), pp. 194–201.

[9] The following works may be mentioned: B. Noack, *Zur johanneischen Tradition* (1954); W. Wilkens, *Die Entstehungsgeschichte des vierten Evangeliums* (1958); R. Gyllenberg, "Die Anfänge der johanneischen Tradition" in *Neutestamentliche Studien für R. Bultmann,* pp. 144–7; S. Schulz, *Untersuchungen zur Menschensohn-Christologie im Johannesevangelium* (1957); C. H. Dodd, *Historical Tradition in the Fourth Gospel* (1964); F. M. Braun, *Jean le Théologien II, les grands traditions d'Israël, l'accord des écritures d'après le quatrième Évangile* (1964); J. A. Bailey, *The Tradition Common to the Gospels of Luke and John* (1963); F. Mussner, " 'Kultische' Aspekte im johanneischen Christusbild", *loc. cit.;* D. M. Smith, "The Sources of the Gospel of John: An Assessment of the Present State of the Problem" in *New Testament Studies,* 10 (1963/64), pp. 336–51; E. Stauffer, "Historische Elemente im vierten Evangelium" in *Bekenntnis zur Kirche. Festgabe für E. Sommerlath* (1960), pp. 33 ff.; R. E. Brown, "The Problem of Historicity of John" in *The Catholic Biblical Quarterly,* 24 (1962), pp. 1–14. The works of F. M. Braun and C. H. Dodd are particularly important; both give a powerful impression of the abundance of Old Testament and early Christian traditions which are made use of in John.

[10] Cf. on this R. Schnackenburg, "Der Menschensohn im Johannesevangelium" in *New Testament Studies,* 11 (1964/65), pp. 123–37.

[11] Schnackenburg shows this, for example, with the theme of the "Son of man" (see preceding note).

[12] A. von Harnack, "Das 'Wir' in den johanneischen Schriften" in *Sitzungsberichte der preussischen Akademie der Wissenschaften, philosophisch-historische Klasse* (1923), pp. 96–113.

[13] *Einleitung in das Neue Testament,* p. 160; similarly Harnack (p. 109): "The community of the faithful, among whom the author includes himself."

[14] The aorist ἐσκήνωσεν immediately preceding, which looks back to the occurrence of the incarnation of the Logos, makes it extremely

probable that the aorist ἐθεασάμεθα also looks back to a definite circle. The aorist ἐλάβομεν in verse 16 too is retrospective (presumably the "grace of baptism" is meant). Besides, the θεᾶσθαι must be judged on the basis of the Johannine act of vision.

[15] Wikenhauser also says on this passage, "The greater probability is that in the "We" it is eyewitnesses of Jesus's activity who are speaking. In addition we may observe that John never attributes this "seeing" to the believing community (cf. above, p. 23).

[16] What M. Heidegger has to say (in *Sein und Zeit,* p. 155) about expression as "communication, utterance", applies here. "It permits sharing in the seeing of what . . . has been disclosed. This shares with another the being which has been disclosed in a definite respect . . . in that world out of which as basis what has been disclosed is met with",—in John's case the world of faith. "What is expressed, as communicated, can be shared with the speaker by others without their having in tangible and visible proximity the being which is disclosed and specified. What is expressed can be further expressed. The circle of those who mutually share in seeing widens out." The "We"-circle of the apostolic eye-witnesses through their "communication" accepted and appropriated in faith becomes the wider "We"-circle of the believing Church. With John, however, the formula primarily applies to the fellowship of apostolic eye-witnesses and hearers.

[17] The heretic, however, who does not abide in the "teaching about Christ" handed down by the apostolic "We"-circle (cf. 2 Jn 9), expresses his independent private gnosis verbally by saying in the singular: ἔγνωκα αὐτόν (cf. 1 Jn 2:4).

[18] Cf. also H. G. Gadamer, "Vom Zirkel des Verstehens" in *Festschrift für M. Heidegger zum 70. Geburtstag* (1959), pp. 24–34; R. Bultmann, "Das Problem der Hermeneutik" in *Glauben und Verstehen, Gesammelte Aufsätze,* II (1952), pp. 211–35.

[19] *Sein und Zeit,* pp. 142 f.

[20] *Ibid.,* p. 148.

[21] *Ibid.,* p. 152.

[22] *Ibid.,* p. 150.

[23] *Ibid.,* p. 153.

[24] Cf. above p. 14.

[25] As a classic example of such "progressive" interpretation we might

point to the (gnostic) Acts of John; the Christ they present regards himself as raised high above the *Christus passus* of apostolic tradition; cf. Acts of John, §§ 97 ff. The statement in § 99 is particularly characteristic: "What I am not, I have been taken for; who I am not, that I was for many others."

[26] Cf. also C. H. Dodd, "Le Kerygma apostolique dans le quatrième évangile" in *Revue d'histoire et de philosophie religieuses*, 31 (1951), pp. 265–74.

[27] *Jean le Théologien*, II (1964).

[28] Cf. also my essay, " 'Kultische' Aspekte im johanneischen Christusbild", *loc. cit.*, and note 8 above.

[29] *Wahrheit und Methode*, p. 252.

[30] *Ibid.*, p. 277.

[31] Cf. in particular Gadamer, *op. cit.*, pp. 261 ff.; and also F. Theunis, "Hermeneutik, Verstehen und Tradition" in *Herméneutique et Tradition. Actes du Colloque International Rome* (1963), pp. 263–82.

[32] Cf. 8:51–5; 14:15, 21, 23; 15:10, 20; 17:6; 1 Jn 2:3–5; 3:22 f.; 5:3, 18.

[33] Cf. Gadamer, *op. cit.*, pp. 266 f.

[34] *Ibid.*, pp. 274 f.

[35] *Ibid.*, p. 275.

[36] This also applies to the Logos-Christology of the fourth gospel, which in fact introduces no alien element into the previous tradition concerning Christ, which always of course saw in Jesus the living word of God (cf. on this G. Kittel in *TWNT*, IV, pp. 126 ff.).

[37] *Wahrheit und Methode*, p. 275.

[38] Further detail on this in VII, 3.

[39] *Wahrheit und Methode*, p. 278.

[40] *Ibid.*, p. 279.

[41] What this means in regard to inspiration will be discussed in section VIII.

[42] Cf. Section II, 2 above.

[43] *Wahrheit und Methode*, p. 282.

[44] *Ibid.*, p. 374.

[45] *Ibid.*, p. 375. The significance of this for the question of the historical Jesus as John sees it will be discussed in Section VII.

[46] *Ibid.*, p. 378.

[47] "Verkündigung und Tradition" in *Evangelische Theologie,* 24 (1964), pp. 565–86 (578 f.).

[48] "Die historische und theologische Tragweite der heutigen Evangelienforschung" in *Zeitschrift für Katholische Theologie,* 86 (1964) pp. 385–417 (390). Cf. also R. Schnackenburg, "Zum Verfahren der Urkirche bei ihrer Jesusüberlieferung" in *Der historische Jesus und der kerygmatische Christus* (1960), pp. 439–54; W. Trilling, "Jesusüberlieferung und apostolische Vollmacht" in *Trierer Theologische Zeitschrift,* 71 (1962), pp. 352–68. In the Instruction of the Pontifical Biblical Commission on the historical truth of the gospels (21 April 1964), three stages of tradition are distinguished "in which Jesus's teaching and life have come down to us"; there is the historical situation in the life of Jesus; the postpaschal situation of apostolic preaching which is characterized by the "fuller understanding which they enjoyed through the impression made by the glorious events concerning Christ and through the illumination of the Spirit of truth"; and the committing to writing of the apostolic tradition about Jesus by the evangelists. The important thing about this Instruction is that the form-history method of exegesis of the gospels is recognized as a legitimate scientific method and that the influence of the situation of postpaschal preaching on the shaping of tradition is acknowledged.

SECTION VII

[1] "Die Sprache des Christus. Sprachliche Beobachtungen an den synoptischen Herrenworten" in *BZ,* new series, 2 (1958), pp. 54–84.

[2] Cf. also the article by R. Schnackenburg: "Ich-Aussagen" in *LTK,* V, cols. 594 f.

[3] But this can only be spoken of in a limited sense, as J. Blank emphasizes (*op. cit.,* pp. 96–99); cf. also E. Haenchen in *TLZ,* 89 (1964), pp. 891 f.

[4] Further details on this in Feine, Behm and Kümmel, *Einleitung in das Neue Testament,* pp. 149–57. Bultmann's pupil H. Becker, for example, attempts in his dissertation, *Die Reden des Johannesevangeliums und der Stil der gnostischen 'Offenbarungsrede'* (1956), to

explain the "style" of the Johannine Christ's discourses by the style of the gnostic 'revelation discourse', but with little success (cf. on this H. Haenchen in *TLZ*, 89 (1964), pp. 883 f.).

[5] The Johannine Christ also brings this to mind by the fact that, according to 14:10, it is the Father "who dwells in me and does his works" (cf. also 4:34; 5:36; 9:3; 10:32; 17:4).

[6] Cf. the all too brief excursus in E.Pax, *EPIΦANEIA. Ein religions-geschichtlicher Beitrag zur biblischen Theologie* (1955), pp. 214–6.

[7] Cf. also H. Kahlefeld, *Die Epiphanie des Erlösers im Johannesevangelium* (1954).

[8] And linguistic interpretation is according to Gadamer "the form of interpretation generally" (*Wahrheit und Methode*, p. 376). In it one's own terminology is hardly to be avoided if it is to be a case of genuine interpretation. "To wish to avoid one's own terms in interpretation is not only impossible but plain contradiction" (*ibid.*, pp. 374 f.). A mere reproduction would be no interpretation; the hermeneutical situation would not be attained; the questions to which an answer is expected would remain unanswered. John's genius consists in his having used in his interpretation a terminology which is perfectly appropriate to the course of the Christ-event and which to a certain extent was determined by the nature of the occurrence itself.

[9] *Wahrheit und Methode*, p. 359.

[10] Cf. K. Kundsin, *Topologische Uberlieferungsstoffe im Johannesevangelium* (1925), pp. 11 f.

[11] *Die Erhöhung und Verherrlichung Jesu im Johannesevangelium* (1960).

[12] *Ibid.*, p. 201.

[13] *Ibid.*, p. 202.

[14] *Ibid.*, p. 203.

[15] *Ibid.*, p. 204.

[16] Cf. also J. Blank, *op. cit.*, p. 140: "It seems that in John's gospel this idea of 'Christ proclaiming himself' was carried through most consistently and forms one of the fundamental structural features of the gospel generally". The identity of the historical and the glorified Christ is, from the ontological point of view, given by what Jesus Christ himself was. This does not mean, of course, that John had no idea of the contrast between the operation of the earthly Jesus and that of the

risen Christ (cf. E. Haenchen in *TLZ*, 89 [1964], pp. 893 f.). For the Church, the identity of the historical and the glorified Christ became evident and conscious by the operation of the Paraclete.

[17] It is unnecessary in the present context to go into the question to what extent the Johannine language, ideas and imagery originated in "Johannine" communities. It would scarcely be possible to give a satisfactory answer in view of the striking uniformity of the world of Johannine language. At all events it is impossible to rate too highly the personal share of the evangelist in his work, including its linguistic side. Cf. on this E. Ruckstuhl, *Die literarische Einheit des Johannesevangeliums* (1951).

[18] *TLZ*, 89 (1964), p. 895.

[19] *Ibid.*

SECTION VIII

[1] Cf. in particular the article by A. Bea on "Inspiration" in *LTK*, V, cols. 703–8, with bibliography; K. Rahner, *Über die Schriftinspiration,* Quaestiones disputatae I (²1959), E. T.: *Inspiration in the Bible* (²1964); K. Rahner, "Inspiration" in *Handbuch theologischer Grundbegriffe*, I (1962), pp. 715–25, with bibliography; J. L. McKenzie, "The Social Character of Inspiration" in *The Catholic Biblical Quarterly*, 24 (1962), pp. 115–23; P. Grelot, "L'inspiration scripturaire" in *Recherches de science religieuse,* 51 (1963), pp. 337–82; P. Benoit, "Révélation et inspiration selon la Bible, chez S. Thomas et dans les discussions modernes" in *Revue Biblique*, 70 (1963), pp 321–70; N. Lohfink, "Über die Irrtumslosigkeit und Einheit der Schrift" in *Stimmen der Zeit,* 174 (1964), pp 161–81.

[2] *LTK,* V, col. 705.

[3] *Handbuch theologischer Grundbegriffe,* I, p. 719.

[4] Cf. for example S. Schulz, *Komposition und Herkunft der Johanneischen Reden* (1960), pp. 182–7. But everything here is still quite hypothetical.

[5] *LTK*, V, col. 1104.

[6] *Die Epiphanie des Erlösers im Johannesevangelium* (1954), p. 78.

INDEX OF JOHANNINE PASSAGES

INDEX OF AUTHORS

CARMELITE MONASTERY
Beckley Hill
Barre, Vt., 05641

DATE BORROWED